Just Don't Lose the Money

Just Don't Lose the Money

By Richard L. Rubino, J.D.

& Samuel J. Liang

www.AcanthusPublishing.com

Published by Acanthus Publishing,
a division of The Ictus Group, LLC
343 Commercial Street
Unit 214, Union Wharf
Boston, MA 02109

Publisher's Cataloging-In-Publication Data
(Prepared by The Donohue Group, Inc.)

Rubino, Richard L.
   Just don't lose the money / by Richard L. Rubino & Samuel J. Liang.

   p. : charts ; cm.

   ISBN: 978-0-9799949-8-2

1. Finance, Personal. 2. Saving and investment. I. Liang, Samuel J. II. Title.

HG179 .R835 2008
332.024/01

Acknowledgments

We would like to thank our families for all the support they have given us throughout the years, especially our wives – Sam's wife Eileen and Rich's wife Winnie. Without them we would not have the success — both family- and business-wise — that we enjoy today.

We would also like to thank our staff — John Conley, Nancy Shannon, Bobbi Ruggiero-Hickey and Cara Szeghy — who keep us organized and make us look good every working day.

Table of Contents

Foreword

Our first book, *No Blood, No Money: How to Make It, How to Keep It, and How to Pass It On to Your Loved Ones,* written in 2005, discussed the basics of estate planning. It described and explained how basic legal documents, such as a power of attorney, a health care proxy, a living will and different types of trusts work, fit into the overall goal of having an efficient way to pass assets to loved ones. The writing of *No Blood, No Money* was motivated by our observation that many people did not have a basic understanding of how legal docments can be used to make sure their wishes are carried out. The book explained things in simple terms so the average person can understand and make informed choices on how best to proceed with an estate plan.

No Blood, No Money, now in its third printing, includes an expanded section on Veterans Benefits and a special chapter titled "Strategies that Work."

The writing of *Just Don't Lose the Money* evolved from our observations on money. Many people are unclear on how different financial vehicles work and need help in knowing where to begin. Many "experts" take it for granted that most people "know the basics." We take nothing for granted and explain how all financial vehicles work. We feel this allows people to better understand what is right for them.

Some of the basics of *Just Don't Lose the Money* are: knowing what you have and how it works, how inflation will cut into your spendable income, how to receive income during retirement, how real estate investments work and much, much more. All explanations are easy to understand and have a *Just Don't Lose the Money* comment.

Each week for the last 8 years, we have been heard on numerous greater Boston radio stations. During our show, "Protecting Your Wealth," we answer questions from listeners that pertain to retirement planning, getting income, protecting assets and using different types of trusts. "Just don't lose the money" is a theme we have used for years and it involves both legal and financial strategies that help save and protect assets.

Although my partner, Sam, is 20 years younger than me and his family is of Chinese descent and mine is of Italian descent, our childhoods were very similar. They revolved around family, savings, no debt, being careful about how you spend, not wasting anything, safety, and just don't lose the money.

When I first got into business, my father, Anthony, had recently passed away. He had handled all the financial matters in the household. He worked full-time, (my mother worked full-time bringing up my brother, sister and me) and he paid all the bills, saved and invested the money. He left my mother financially secure. After gathering all the assets they had accumulated, she needed help with managing those assets, and she needed a plan so she would have income for the rest of her life. When I told her, "Mom, I am in the business now. I will help you take care of your money," she said to me, "Richard, I love you and trust you. You can do whatever you think is best, **just don't lose the money.**" The title of our book was born from that phrase. My mom was 62 years old when my father died, she is now 92 and has more money than she started with.

Just Don't Lose the Money is more than just about money. Although we talk about money all the time, it is a broad philosophy that includes legal, tax, and safe money strategies. Losing money in the stock market and losing money to pay for estate tax is the same dollar lost.

Many in the financial business take it for granted that people know the basics, and we have come to find out that this is not the case. *Just Don't Lose the Money* is designed to inform you of these basics—what they are and how they work. *Just Don't Lose the Money* covers basics from bank accounts, CDs, mutual funds, individual stocks, annuities, and much more. It explains in clear understandable language how things work and whether or not they are safe, and how safe they really are. It talks about risk in all aspects of your financial life—risk in growing assets, risks in getting income from assets and risk in the distribution of assets to heirs. All risk can be either eliminated or reduced—that's what *Just Don't Lose the Money* is about.

You must remember that an estate plan or portfolio design should change as your circumstances change. A 30 year old does not, and should not, have the same estate plan and financial positions that an 80 year old has. There is a transition that must be made over time and one's risk level should be reduced with time. So, the *Just Don't Lose the Money* philosophy is a moving target.

We hope you enjoy this book and that you don't lose the money you've worked so hard for. Remember our mantra, *Just Don't Lose the Money.*

What Do You Have to Lose and What Do You Want to Gain?

When my wife, Winnie, was listening to our radio show one week, she heard me comment on a letter we received. "It is important to know what you have," I said. "We will send you one of our organizer kits so you can keep track." Winnie asked me, "Why don't we have an organizer kit?" It was like the shoe maker's son having no shoes. Well, now we have our own organizer kit. In our family, I handle the long-term financial and legal picture. Winnie does everything else. It was important for both of us to have a full picture of assets and legal documents. Follow the instructions in this chapter and get organized.

You have worked hard all these years to earn what you've got. Damned hard. Right now you're probably shaking your head and smiling ruefully, saying that you wish it were so but really, whatever wealth you have accumulated is just due to luck or fate. Hogwash. Even if you started out with a family fortune, there is no way that fortune lasted all these years without hard work and discipline on your part.

Okay, we've gotten past the roadblock of false modesty. But before a true conversation about how not to lose what you've spent a lifetime accumulating can take place, we have one more roadblock to circumvent. Namely, our culture's pronounced aversion to discussing money in any way, shape, or form.

Incredibly enough, in a thoroughly capitalist society where people routinely admit to every conceivable personal indiscretion on national television, talking about money is one of the last remaining social taboos. For many people, this taboo even extends to thinking about money. Making money a top concern is often seen as a character flaw, a sign that your priorities are out of order, that you care more about material matters than about family, health, or other personal matters.

Double hogwash. While constantly discussing financial matters will quickly leave you isolated in a corner at cocktail parties, there is nothing wrong with having an in-depth conversation about money in the proper time and place, like when you're trying to create a plan to avoid losing your hard-earned life savings.

And there is no better way to show concern for your family, your health, or your personal life than to make money a top priority. What shows more love and care for your family members: a well-designed estate plan that protects the majority of your assets, or a laissez-faire approach to inheritance that puts half of your hard-earned wealth in the hands of the taxman? What shows a more health-conscious approach to life: getting an ironclad insurance policy that will pay for your lifetime medical needs, or crossing your fingers and hoping you never get really sick or seriously injured? What shows more concern for a family: a plan that passes assets under ANY circumstances or again just crossing your fingers? As for hobbies and other important personal pleasures of life, aren't they easier to enjoy without interference from the stress and anxiety caused by unpaid bills and mounting debt?

Okay, we've gotten past the second major roadblock to having a serious financial discussion. It's perfectly okay to devote time, a lot of time, to talking and thinking about your money—how to earn it, how to keep it, how to protect it from avoidable taxes, fees and penalties, and how to pass it on to surviving loved ones rather than to the government or nursing home after your death.

Oh yeah, one more roadblock we need to plow right on through. Nobody likes to talk or think about death, and with good reason. But without some foresight and planning, your personal death will also result in the death of your estate, at least from your family's point of view. You don't have to contemplate the time or nature of your demise, just what you need to do to ensure your assets are well protected when it happens.

Now that's all been settled, let's take a deep breath and exhale. Phew. Doesn't that feel better? We've gotten all the reflexive resistance to talking and thinking about money out of our system. So let's get down to business—the business of not losing your money.

Just Don't Lose the Money is more than a clever title. It's a whole way of thinking about your assets, which include money and monetary instruments as well as property and other valuables. It's taking a safe, steady approach to saving and growing your wealth. It's understanding that in the long run, a guaranteed five percent return is a whole lot better than an unpredictable return that may be 20 percent but may also be zero or even a big loss. It's realizing that while nobody can completely avoid taxes (at least not legally), there are easy steps you can take to delay and minimize them. It's knowing the difference between acceptable risk and risk that is downright foolhardy. It's taking advantage of certain legal strategies that help save money like using Revocable Trusts to avoid probate, Medicaid Protective Trusts to shield assets from nursing home costs, and Irrevocable Life Insurance Trusts to avoid estate taxes.

The first step to not losing your money is figuring out exactly what you have to lose. Sounds simple enough, but how many people can honestly tell you their net worth off the top of their heads? Maybe they can tell you their salary, or the size of their retirement plan, or the value of their house, but these are all pieces of a much bigger financial puzzle.

To determine your net worth, start by identifying all of your assets and income sources. In many cases, you may be holding something that represents both an asset and an income source. For example, the principal and accumulated interest on an IRA represents an asset, while an IRA's distributions (if you are taking them) represent an income source. A list of typical assets and income sources begins on the next page.

Typical Assets

Bank Savings – Principal and accumulated interest on checking and savings accounts, Certificates of Deposit, Money Market Funds, etc.

Retirement Accounts – Principal and accumulated interest on IRA, 401(k), pension, SEP (Simplified Employee Pension), etc.

Fixed/Variable Annuities – Principal and accumulated interest on annuities purchased from insurance companies.

Stocks/Bonds/Mutual Funds – Principal and accumulated interest on these investment vehicles.

Real Estate – Property you own for personal or commercial use.

Valuables/Collectibles – Items such as antiques, artwork, precious metals, automobiles, furniture, large appliances, collectible memorabilia, etc.

Trusts – Legal entities that allow you to hold and manage tangible, intangible, and real estate property while sheltering it from certain tax or nursing home liabilities.

Insurance – Principal and accumulated interest of insurance policies, as well as surrender value if applicable.

TYPICAL INCOME SOURCES

Salary – Wages from full- or part-time work.

Social Security/Disability – Fixed monthly payments for qualifying participants of these government-funded programs.

Bank Savings - Withdrawals and redemptions of principal and interest from different types of bank accounts.

Retirement Accounts – Distributions and withdrawals of principal and interest from IRA, 401(k), pension, SEP, etc.

Fixed/Variable Annuities – Distributions of principal and interest of annuities.

Stocks/Bonds/Mutual Funds – Dividends and distributions from these investment vehicles.

Real Estate – Rental income from commercial real estate.

Trusts – Beneficiaries of trusts may receive distributions, especially common for named beneficiaries of estate trusts.

Just Don't Lose the Money Tip
Get a Handle on What You Have

If you haven't done so already, hopefully this chapter has inspired you to take a thorough accounting of all your assets, income sources, and liabilities to determine your true net worth. But now is not the time to rest on your laurels! Finances are highly fluid, and today's asset could be tomorrow's liability, or vice versa.

To enable continuous tracking of your net worth, set up a spreadsheet that contains information such as names of financial institutions, account numbers, asset or liability types, and dollar amounts. Review and update this spreadsheet at least once a year.

MONEY CHART (ASSETS)

#	Name of Account	Qualified Plan (Y/N)	Account No.	Company	12/31/_____ Value
1					
2					
3					
4					
5					

6

7

8

9

10

11

12

13

14

15

16

Total: _____

MONEY CHART (INCOME)

#	Income Source	Your Income	Spouse's Income	Total Annual Income
1	Social Security			
2	Employer Pension Plans			
3	IRAs/401K Distribution			
4	Annuities			
5	Other			
6				
7				
8				
9				
10				
11				
12				

Total: _____

Notes: Last year spending _____

These lists are not necessarily exhaustive; there are numerous methods of obtaining, saving, and building assets. But they provide a good general idea of the kinds of things you should consider when adding up the "plus" side of your net worth ledger. Of course, the whole idea of "net" worth is that it represents your total worth after deducting all expenses and liabilities. These are much less fun to calculate, but no less important in figuring out exactly where you stand financially. A list of typical expenses and liabilities begins on the next section.

TYPICAL EXPENSES AND LIABILITIES

Taxes – Federal, state, and local taxes represent the single biggest threat to your personal assets. Taxes can destroy the value of the smartest, highest-return investment if they are not properly accounted and planned for. Naturally, we all want to pay our fair share toward keeping the country running, but why pay more than your fair share if you don't have to?

Mortgage/Rent – Outside of taxes, mortgage and rent payments often represent the biggest single expense of most people. Quite simply, mortgage and rent represent the "cost of living." Unlike taxes, mortgage and rent are unavoidable unless you own a piece of property outright or have an extremely generous relative or friend who can provide you with a free roof over your head. For the rest of us, mortgage and/or rent is a fact of financial life that must be taken into careful account when determining expenses and net worth. A worthy goal is to eliminate your mortgage ten years prior to retirement.

10

Food – What could be more elementary than the cost of nourishment? In a country of plenty like the U.S., food goes well beyond nourishment and is a staple of recreation and entertainment. When figuring out your annual food bill, make sure to look beyond the weekly grocery tab and also look at how often you eat out or host a special occasion. That daily cup of coffee or weekly round of drinks at the neighborhood pub? They count as part of your food expenses, too.

Utilities – Not just electricity, heat, and home phone, but also cable, Internet, cell phone, and any other personal service that has been invented since this book went to press. Energy costs have risen sharply in the past few years, and this increase should be accounted for when thinking about utility expenses.

Education – Societal trends toward marrying or remarrying, and having families later in life means that many people now have college-aged children as they approach or enter their retirement years. Those of you who had kids at a younger age are hardly off the hook, because now you probably have grandkids who could use a helping hand (preferably reaching into a helping wallet) in paying for their college education. Along with medical expenses and energy costs, educational expenses have spiraled well past the rate of inflation and show no signs of slowing down anytime soon.

Insurance – Prudent forethought and planning are at the heart of the *Just Don't Lose the Money* mindset. Properly insuring your life, your health, your home, your auto, and any other valuables you own is a necessity. Keep in mind that medical costs will likely increase with age, and government programs like Medicare and Medicaid can hardly be counted on to cover all your healthcare costs. This expense is hardly cheap, but well worth it. Often overlooked is Umbrella Insurance, which covers liabilities that are above the limits of your other insurance policies.

Uninsured Medical Bills – Insurance may not cover certain procedures or treatments, pay more than a certain amount, or pay until a deductible kicks in. The bill is still there to be paid, and nobody else is stepping up to pay it for you.

Credit Card/Personal Loan Debt – Americans carry a staggering load of debt tied to credit cards and personal loans. How much of that burden do you share? Just a tip—when you get the bill, pay it in full!

Transportation – This includes monthly car loan payments, fuel expenses, auto maintenance and repairs, as well as the cost of public transportation.

Just Don't Lose the Money Tip
Figure Your Annual Expenses

Determining your net worth is great, but that information will go to waste if you don't actively apply it to your everyday life. Once you reach age 50, your habits have been formed—either you're a spender, a saver, or somewhere in the middle. In order to prepare for your retirement needs, just add up all you spend each year by going through your check register for the past two years (deduct any one time expenses). This exercise will give you a good idea of what your "burn rate" will be when you retire.

Compare the cost of your annual expenses each year, keeping in mind that you will need to maintain roughly 90 percent of your pre-retirement income in your post-retirement years and that your savings need to outlive you. Make adjustments if necessary, cutting or scaling back the most frivolous expenses first.

BURN RATE CHART

Expenses	Year									
	20__	20__	20__	20__	20__	20__	20__	20__	20__	20__
Federal Taxes										
State Taxes										
Local/Property Taxes										
Mortgage/Rent										
Food										
Utilities										
Education										
Insurance										
Uninsured Medical Bills										
Credit Card Interest										
Transportation										
Clothing										
Recreation/Gifts/ Misc.										

Total : _____

Clothing – Some people spend more on clothes than others, but we all spend something.

Recreation/Travel/Gifts/Miscellaneous – Everything or everyone else you spend money on. The more grandkids, the more gifts.

Again, these lists are not necessarily designed as a road map on how to live your life. Instead, they will help you get your arms around what is your realistic spending rate.

Compare your income with your outflow ("burn rate"). If you do this each year, you will not be surprised at retirement. Hopefully, you are left with a positive number. If you are left with a number near or at zero, you're scraping by, but a major setback (death of a spouse, debilitating disease or injury, collapse of a major investment holding) would mean major financial trouble. If you're left with a negative number, start cutting and eliminating all expenses and liabilities NOW and see if you can transfer even a little of those savings into a secure, tax-deferred, or tax-free investment vehicle.

What's the number? How much income do you need when you retire?

Let's assume you have a "burn rate" number that you're reasonably comfortable with at first glance. Now it's time to look at your post-retirement goals and see if your "money chart" is really enough to provide you comfort. One discomforting fact to keep in mind: Estimates of how much income you will need to maintain your pre-retirement lifestyle after retiring have risen from 65 to 70 percent of your pre-retirement expenses up to 90 percent of your pre-retirement expenses. People are living longer than they used to. The key is setting goals and managing your assets so that you do not outlive your money. In other words, you need to make sure that your money

14

lasts as long as you do. Consider this: According to MarketWatch, for a married couple both age 65, there is a one in four chance that one of the spouses will live for another 30 years! That means having to make sure that they can potentially live off of their retirement income for that long. You need to plan prudently and cut back where necessary, so you don't have to count on only that Social Security check to see you through!

Everyone's goals in life are different. Personal post-retirement goals cannot be summed up as neatly as assets and liabilities. Nevertheless, on the next page there are some broad goal categories you can look at to determine how much money you will need to make each year after you retire.

POST-RETIREMENT GOALS

Basic Survival – Food, clothing, shelter. The stuff you literally cannot live without. Take a realistic appraisal of these goals. You can subsist on a diet of tomato soup and grilled cheese sandwiches, but how long will you actually stick to it?

Enjoyment of Life Beyond the Necessities – You don't have to rent a place for a week on Martha's Vineyard every summer, but if you've been doing it regularly for the past 30 years, chances are you'll want to keep doing it after you retire. Less extravagantly, you will probably occasionally want to eat a meal in a nice restaurant, visit a museum exhibit, or take in a ballgame.

Creating an Inheritance – Most of us possess an instinctive drive to leave a legacy behind. Whether you want to ensure that your spouse is well-cared for in his or her later years, help your kids, grandkids, or great-grandkids achieve their dreams, or even donate to a favorite charity or your alma mater, inheritances do not create themselves. You must build and maintain assets to give them life.

Paying for Education, Weddings, and other Major Expenses of Children and Grandchildren during Your Lifetime – Most people pay for at least a portion of their children's college education; and many pay for grandchildren to continue their educational careers after high school. As mentioned previously, the cost of a college education is growing at a rate that far exceeds the pace of inflation. And, of course, many retirees like to help their kids and grandkids out with expenses such as weddings, childbirth, and buying a home. A note on weddings: Historically, the family of the bride has picked up the lion's share of the tab for a wedding, but, in recent years, that tradition has faded somewhat and the family of the groom has been contributing more. Don't assume that having sons is a bulwark against high wedding expenses.

Long-term Medical Care/Nursing Home Expenses – Our longer lifespans are wonderful, but one consequence is that the need for long-term medical and nursing home care has exploded in recent years. There is a strong chance that at some point in your later years you will need one or both of these services. Without proper planning and sheltering of assets, long-term medical and/or nursing home care can evaporate a net worth of almost any size.

Management of Money and Risk – Effective management of money and financial risk is not for the faint of heart or the untrained. That is why a huge industry of financial service professionals exists to help you manage your money and other assets. This help is generally not cheap, but the rule of "you get what you pay for" definitely applies.

So now you've figured out your goals. Look at your "money chart" again and see if you can realistically meet your aspirations. The first step is to make sure that your goals lie within your means and that your expenses are equal to or less than your savings and income. If they don't, you need to either scale back your expectations for the future, increase your means, or do a combination of both. There is nothing wrong with a little scaling back, either. A yearly excursion to a local beach can be just as relaxing as a week on the Vineyard, and Junior can always attend a state college or take out some student loans to help defray the cost of his college education!

A QUICK REVIEW

At the end of each chapter, we will conduct a quick review of some of the key points made. This will help you remember the most important things and above all, set you on the path to not losing the money!

1 *Just Don't Lose the Money* is more than a motto, it's a way of thinking about your assets. The best way to make money is to keep it, and protecting your assets does more to promote growth than risking them on chancy schemes with faint hopes of a high pay-off. As is true in most parts of life, slow and steady is the best path to long-term success when it comes to managing your assets.

2 Develop your Money Chart of assets/liabilities and Burn Rate Chart of income/expenses as shown. This exercise helps you keep track of how you're doing.

3 Determine your main post-retirement goals and try to figure out what it will cost you each year to achieve them. Assume that you will need to pay 90 percent of your current expenses to maintain a suitable lifestyle after retirement.

Sweet Certainty
Fixed-Return Investments

Safe is not necessarily safe. Why? Because of the "hidden tax" - inflation. Keeping all your money in the bank can be detrimental because of taxes and inflation. Fixed investments are a must, but they are only a part of the piece.

Any serious attempt at investment planning needs to begin with some serious self-examination. We're not talking about the kind of self-examination that leads to a greater understanding of one's place in the cosmos or how everything fits together. Hopefully, you got that out of the way during late-night bull sessions with your buddies back in the 1960s and 70s.

Rather, we're talking about the kind of self-examination that leads to a greater understanding of how much risk you are willing to take versus how much potential return you are seeking to gain. Broadly speaking, the more at risk an investment places your money, the higher potential return it can deliver. Naturally, this means that investments which promise the chance to make an obscene amount of profit in a short time also promise the chance to lose most or all of the money you put into them just as quickly (if not more quickly).

Given the title of and mindset advocated by this book, you can probably guess that, on the whole, we would urge you to shy away from the "make you or break you" investment opportunities that exist out there. They are rarely a good idea and as you near or enter the retirement stage of your career, they become downright dangerous.

However, this hardly means that we encourage you to take no risks at all. There are plenty of low- to moderate-risk investment opportunities with enough potential upside to fit well within a portfolio built around *Just Don't Lose the Money* principles. The chances of your losing everything you put into them are low, and even if the worst does happen, as long as they are integrated into a larger, well-rounded investment plan, you can absorb the loss without jeopardizing everything you have spent your life creating. The next chapter covers how to select and manage variable return investments in a *Just Don't*

Lose the Money-approved manner.

This chapter looks at the safest investments of all: fixed-return investments. These secure investment vehicles offer negligible risk of losing your money, but in return for that security, offer a relatively low rate of guaranteed interest. They also usually offer fewer tax advantages than variable-return investments.

We do not recommend that anyone build a portfolio exclusively consisting of fixed-return investments, but we do advise that a portion of your investment dollars be allocated to fixed-return investments. This will help balance the risk created by your variable-return investment selections. To determine the exact mix of fixed- and variable-return investments that best suits your long-term financial needs and risk comfort zone, consult a professional financial advisor. The following is an overview of some of the most common fixed-return investment vehicles available on the market today.

MONEY IN THE BANK

The fixed-return investment vehicle that is most familiar, and that virtually everyone participates in, is the bank account. A bank invests the money you place in your account at what it hopes will be a much higher interest rate than what it pays you for keeping the account. The Federal Deposit Insurance Corporation (FDIC), a U.S. government corporation, insures all deposits in checking and savings accounts up to $100,000 per depositor.

Even if your bank defaults or closes, any money you have invested in checking, savings, or certain other types of accounts is guaranteed up to $100,000. That's why a sure thing is often referred to as "money in the bank." Since the start of FDIC insurance on January 1, 1934, no depositor has lost a single cent of insured funds as a result of a bank failure. However, the interest rates paid on bank accounts, particularly on interest-earning checking and savings accounts, may be below the rate of inflation.

Having a healthy bank account is key to maintaining a fluid cash flow, but you never want to have your bank account serve as your primary or sole investment vehicle. (You'd be amazed for how many people this is the case!) Banks offer investors several different vehicles to choose from:

Just Don't Lose the Money Tip
Diversify Your Fixed Return Investments

While it is important to hold some fixed return investments to ensure that you will keep what you've made (as opposed to exposing it to risk for potential high growth), it is just as important that you not put all your financial eggs in one fixed-return basket. Invest in a variety of fixed-return instruments.

Besides the standard savings and checking accounts, open a CD and a fixed annuity, and perhaps purchase some U.S. Savings Bonds. You can also time the maturities of your fixed-income investments to come due in conjunction with different major life events (retirement, a child or grandchild entering college, etc.) to provide some guaranteed financial assistance.

Savings Accounts: One of the most basic investment vehicles of them all. Savings accounts typically pay a low fixed annual interest rate. The only way to access funds is to withdraw or transfer them. There may be a minimum balance required to keep the account open. Interest is considered part of your adjusted gross income for federal and state income tax purposes. Also, the interest is generally lower than a bank CD.

Checking Accounts: Checking accounts can be interest-free or interest-earning. Interest-earning accounts will usually apply service charges for going below a minimum balance and may also charge check fees and other fees and penalties. Funds can be drawn by check or debit card at any time, although the full value of the checking account is usually not available. Stiff fees and penalties usually apply to overdrawn checking accounts (i.e., "bouncing" a check). Any interest earned on a checking account is considered part of your adjusted gross income for federal and state income tax purposes.

Certificate of Deposit (CD): A CD is a specific, fixed-term bank deposit that pays a fixed rate of interest above that offered for conventional savings and checking accounts. The specified term varies from three months to five years, with higher interest rates offered for longer terms. Money cannot be withdrawn before the end of the term without penalty, and some CDs automatically rollover, or reinvest the money in a new, identical-term CD if you don't notify the bank of your intent to withdraw or transfer funds within a certain number of days before maturity.

CDs earn interest at an annual rate, which is prorated for shorter-term deposits. You can arrange quarterly or semiannual interest payments on long-term CDs, although by doing so you lose the benefit of compound interest. Any interest earned on a CD is considered part of your adjusted gross income for federal and state income tax purposes. CDs are FDIC-insured, which makes them a safe way to invest money that you won't need for a while at a better interest rate than you can get from a savings or checking account.

Money Market Deposit Account (MMDA): An MMDA is a high-interest, high-minimum-balance deposit account that is designed for savings, but allows the holder limited capability to write checks and perform other transfers. Any interest earned on an MMDA is considered part of your adjusted gross income for federal and state income tax purposes. Fees and penalties are typically high. MMDAs are FDIC-insured, making them another safe option for investing money at an interest rate better than that of savings and checking accounts.

Money Market Funds: Money Market Funds are mutual funds that invest in certain short-term debt instruments. Issued by banks, corporations, and the U.S. Treasury, their market value does not fluctuate and holders can usually write high-minimum checks or redeem shares at will. While Money Market Funds are considered safe investments, they do not carry FDIC insurance. Any interest earned on a Money Market Fund is considered part of your adjusted gross income for federal and state income tax purposes.

ENSURED TAX-DEFERRED GROWTH: FIXED AND FIXED-INDEX ANNUITIES

What if you could make a long-term investment that was approximately as safe as putting money in the bank, and offered the additional bonus of allowing your money to earn tax-deferred interest? In other words, you wouldn't have to pay any tax until the investment paid distributions or reached maturity. Sounds pretty good, right? Welcome to the world of fixed and fixed index annuities.

A fixed tax-deferred annuity is a contract with an insurance company that guarantees your principal plus a minimum rate of interest. You can open an annuity with a single deposit or a series of deposits. Some annuities offer a variable rate of interest; we will investigate those in the next chapter. In this chapter, we will examine fixed annuities, which pay a predetermined rate of annual interest during the life of the contract, and fixed index annuities, which link interest payments to the performance of major stock indices (although not actually invested in that stock index).

Fixed Annuities: In principle, a fixed annuity operates similarly to a CD from a bank. It pays annual interest throughout its duration, usually at a rate better than banks will offer for a CD. Some fixed annuities adjust their interest rates to keep pace with rising inflation. And unlike CDs, interest and earnings of fixed annuities are tax-deferred, which means you do not have to pay taxes until money is withdrawn or the annuity reaches maturity. You can control the amount you withdraw, and whatever amount is withdrawn is subject to tax, each year. The IRS will tack a 10 percent penalty onto any money withdrawn from an annuity before the holder reaches the age of 59 ½.

As the holder of a fixed annuity, you can choose to receive payments at regular intervals once you reach age 59 ½. This is known as "annuitizing" the contract. There are several different methods of annuitizing your contract. A life-only annuity, which provides payments during your life, offers the highest income, but offers no death benefits or surrender value (for more information on surrender values, see the life insurance section of Chapter 9). A life annuity with term certain operates the same as a life-only annuity, except that if you die within the term, your heirs receive your payments until the term ends. An installment refund annuity guarantees you a lifetime income and if you die before collecting the original purchase price, it returns the remainder to your loved ones in installments until it is paid out.

The latest development in the fixed annuity world is a "Fixed Annuity with a Guaranteed Income Option." This type of annuity can create a guaranteed lifetime income stream without "annuitizing" the contract. The guaranteed income option comes with an On/Off switch that allows you to receive a guaranteed minimum lifetime income payment. You can decide whether or not to take this payment on a year-to-year basis. Many times this type of account is used in conjunction with other equity accounts and allows you to choose where to take income from depending on investment performance and tax situation.

Speak with a professional financial advisor before selecting a specific type of fixed annuity. If your primary goal is to create an income to sustain you in your retirement years, a guaranteed minimum lifetime income option annuity may be your best choice. This also will create something of value to pass on to your loved ones. One nice added bonus of annuities is that they pass directly to named beneficiaries and bypass probate (see Chapter 11 to find out more about probate and why you want to avoid it).

Fixed-Index Annuity: A fixed-index annuity links the interest you collect on your principal and earnings to increases in a major stock index such as the Standard & Poor's 500 or Dow Jones. Some fixed-index annuities guarantee a minimum return on your investment, which is a nice protection to have against the inevitable down cycles of the stock market while you still enjoy the full benefits of the up cycles. A fixed index annuity can, in some cases, include a minimum lifetime income option that can be exercised after one year.

By purchasing a fixed index annuity, you are not making any kind of stock purchase. You are simply tying the interest you receive from your fixed annuity to the performance of a particular group of stocks. By investing in a fixed-index annuity with a guaranteed minimum return, your annuity performance can actually beat the performance of the stock market, without risking any of the principal. You can make money in an up market while getting a guaranteed minimum return in a down market. Fixed-index annuities are generally more complex than other types of fixed annuities and you should always consult with a qualified financial professional who is specifically familiar with how they operate before investing in one.

Fixed-index annuity can outperform the S&P 500 because it can only go up and not go down (see chart).

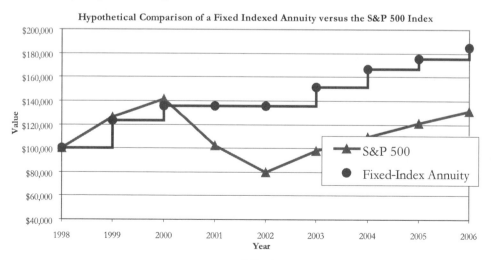

Hypothetical Comparison of a Fixed Indexed Annuity versus the S&P 500 Index

INVESTING IN UNCLE SAM

Although most bonds technically represent a "fixed" investment since they offer a consistent interest rate on your principal, they can be bought and sold at a fluctuating market value and consequently carry some default risk. These types of bonds are covered with the other variable return investment vehicles discussed in Chapter 3. One exception to this rule is the U.S. Savings Bond.

U.S. Savings Bond: By investing in U.S. Savings Bonds, you are investing in the full faith and credit of the U.S. government. This makes payment of interest and principal on a U.S. Savings Bond as safe as it is in an FDIC-insured bank account. No market exists for U.S. Savings Bonds, as you can cash them or give them as a gift or inheritance, but you cannot resell them. Interest is exempt from state and local tax, and federal taxes can either be paid each year as interest accrues or in-full upon cashing-in, disposal, or maturity.

As with other secure government-backed investment vehicles, the return on U.S. Savings Bonds is low. However, many people find them useful, secure methods of saving for future expenses such as a college education (see Chapter 7).

A QUICK REVIEW

1 While the *Just Don't Lose the Money* investment approach doesn't involve eliminating all financial risk, it does involve constructing a portfolio that includes secure, fixed-return investments. By creating a proper mix of these vehicles with low- to moderate-risk variable-return vehicles such as stocks, bonds, and mutual funds, you can maximize your investment return for an acceptable amount of financial risk.

2 Banks offer a variety of FDIC-insured deposits that provide interest rates that generally go up the longer you commit to keeping your money in place. Traditional savings and checking accounts are key to maintaining cash flow, but are a poor choice to hold as your primary or sole investment vehicles.

3 Fixed annuities and fixed-index annuities are a secure way to invest your money at a fixed rate of return, which is generally better than you will receive from a bank vehicle such as a CD. A fixed annuity is a contract with an insurance company that guarantees you the return of your principal plus earnings and interest, either as a lump sum distribution or in installments. A fixed-index annuity is a special type of fixed annuity that ties its return to the performance of a major stock index. There are several other types of fixed annuities with different payment options, and consulting a professional financial advisor is strongly advised before investing in any annuity product.

Nothing Ventured, Nothing Gained
Variable-Return Investments

Every financial vehicle is designed to work a certain way. Variable returns and investments can go up and down. If they are down AND you have to take money out, your portfolio has less of a chance to recover. Each type of investment is designed for a different purpose. An income portfolio does not look like a growth portfolio. Would you use your convertible to haul rocks and sand? No. You would use a dump truck. Both are vehicles but are designed for different uses. It is the same with money.

Now that we've examined fixed-return investments, it's time to turn the magnifying glass toward variable-return investments. These investment vehicles produce a yield based partially or wholly on their fluctuating market value, which may or may not be the same as their actual value. Stock market tycoons such as Warren Buffett have amassed great fortunes by identifying and investing in stocks that the market has undervalued, and anyone who got burned in the turn-of-the-century dotcom boom has learned the perils of overvalued stocks first-hand.

As a prudent *Just Don't Lose the Money* investor, you're not looking for that single investment to put you over the top, and you're certainly not looking for an investment whose bottom will drop out once a particular fad has passed. What you are looking for is a low- to moderate-risk investment vehicle that will allow you a reasonable chance for steady growth beyond what your more secure fixed-rate investments will provide.

Now that you know how to go about building the fixed-rate portion of your portfolio, it's time to learn the basics of the major products available to fill the variable-rate portion of your portfolio. Again, we cannot stress strongly enough how important it is to meet with a professional financial advisor to determine what level of risk is acceptable to you and what mix of variable-rate investments will best suit your individual financial and personal goals.

In this chapter, we will review five basic variable-rate investment vehicles: stocks, bonds, mutual funds, Exchange Traded Funds (ETF), and variable annuities.

Owning Your Share

A stock represents a share of ownership in a corporation. By issuing and distributing shares of stock, corporations raise financial capital. For the purposes of this discussion, we will focus on common stock, which gives the holder voting rights in corporate decisions. Stocks are traded on the major exchanges such as the New York Stock Exchange and NASDAQ. You have to buy and sell stocks through a broker or an online service and pay a commission on the transaction.

Historically, owning shares of an individual stock provides the best long-term return of any investment you can make. For example, large-company stocks gained on average 10.4% from 1926 to 2005. In the short-term, however, prices of individual stocks are highly volatile and extremely difficult to predict.

The major drawback to investing large sums of money into shares of one or a few individual stocks is that your risk is concentrated in a narrow area. One way to affordably diversify your stock holdings is to invest in shares of a mutual fund, a vehicle that pools investors' money to invest in a range of stocks. We will discuss mutual funds in more detail later on in this chapter.

If you do want to invest in stock shares of individual companies, here is a quick primer on some of the jargon you will hear often. Earnings represent net income after taxes and funds set aside for preferred stock dividends divided by the number of common shares outstanding. They equal growth. The price/earnings ratio (or P/E ratio) is the current price of a stock divided by earnings of either the past 12 months (trailing P/E ratio) or by the estimated earnings of the next 12 months (anticipated P/E ratio). New, fast-growing companies tend to have high P/E ratios and are also more volatile.

Book value is the difference between a company's assets and liabilities. Return on book is total net income represented as a percentage of a stock's book value. Total return is the sum of a stock's price changes plus current income; and debt equity ratio is a way of measuring a stock's financial health by dividing book value by debts. Past volatility is a number representing how a particular stock's value has fluctuated compared to the movement in a specific stock index.

Owning shares of an individual stock does have its advantages. As opposed to participating in a fund where a manager makes investment decisions, you hold all the power to determine when and how much to buy and sell. You owe no taxes on an individual stock until you sell it; then, any profits you make are taxed as either short-term capital gains (stock you've held for a year or less) or long-term capital gains (stock you've held for more than a year). In both cases, capital gains tax rates are relatively low compared to other income sources.

If you lose money in a stock sale, you get to deduct a portion of that capital loss from your adjusted net income. Furthermore, some stocks pay dividends, which are cash or additional shares distributed on a quarterly basis.

Purchasing shares of an individual stock is probably the riskiest variable rate investment you can make. If you do decide to go this route, make sure that only a small percentage of your portfolio is made up of individual stocks and perform lots of careful research before making any purchases.

Definitely avoid buying stocks of new or little-known companies that are "hot"; this is a short-term strategy with little chance of success over the long haul. It's better to buy shares of established companies that you can be reasonably certain will still be paying dividends and offering resale value for years to come.

Timing is Everything

Individual stocks can be extremely volatile, and timing is critical in terms of gains and losses. For example, take Yahoo, one of the dot-com sector's high-flyers. The timing of your purchase and subsequent sale could have caused you to enjoy huge gains or suffer huge losses. If you purchased Yahoo in June 1997, when it was selling for $35.25/share, and sold it in January 2000 during the crest of the dot-com boom at $322.06/share, you would have realized a gain of $286.81/share or over 800%! However, if you purchased Yahoo in January 2000 at $322.06/share and held it until June 2007, when it was valued at $27.31, you would have lost $294.75/share or 91% of your initial investment! As the saying goes, "You gotta know when to hold 'em and know when to fold 'em..."

INVESTING IN DEBT

Investing in the debt of a private company or government entity may sound like a strange idea, but that's exactly what bond investors do every day. To be more precise, a bond investor is actually making a loan to the bond issuer and later collecting it with interest, although bonds are generally not referred to as loans.

Because bonds offer a fixed-interest rate, they tend to be a more steady and secure investment than stocks. However, most bonds are bought in the secondary marketplace, where prices vary in face value depending on how the interest rate of the bond compares to the going interest rate. We will explain how to size up the value of a bond in the secondary marketplace shortly.

Generally speaking, bonds perform the opposite of stocks. The bond market will usually rise when interest rates are low, and fall when interest rates go up, which is the converse reaction stocks have to interest rate fluctuations. Thus keeping a mix of both stocks and bonds in your portfolio helps hedge your bets against interest rate changes.

Also, many financial advisors will tell their clients to increase the percentage of bonds in their portfolios as they approach retirement, since bonds tend to offer more security. However, as noted earlier, with people living longer you need to make sure a fixed-return is sufficient so that you do not outlive your money. Of course, you should speak with a financial professional to determine your own unique personal investment needs before making any decisions in regard to buying stocks vs. bonds.

When evaluating a bond, the first thing to look at is the "coupon rate," which is simply the fixed-annual interest rate the bond offers on your investment principal. The coupon rate is known as the yield. The current yield is the annual interest payment measured as a percentage of the bond's current market price. As mentioned earlier, bonds tend to increase in value when interest rates are low. This is because that means there is a good chance a bond can offer a yield above the going interest rate. For example, a bond paying a six percent yield will sell above face value in the secondary marketplace when the going interest rate is four percent and below face value when the going interest rate is eight percent.

Two other factors to evaluate when considering investing in a bond are yield to maturity and yield to call. Yield to maturity measures the estimated eventual gain or loss a current bond owner will incur by holding the bond until maturity. A bond held to maturity is redeemed for its "face value." Yield to call measures the assumed value of a bond if it is called at first call date. Many, but not all bonds, can be "called," or repurchased by the issuer for a premium before maturing.

There are numerous varieties of bonds, which can be issued by private corporations and public agencies as well as by federal, state, and local governments.

Government Bonds: Bonds issued by a state, or local government or government agency are known as municipal bonds (also called "munis"). Municipal bonds are issued to raise capital for general government programs or specific projects such as roads, bridges, or hospitals. General obligation bonds, which are the most common and least risky, are backed by the full taxing power of the government agency that issued them. Other munis may only be backed by the revenue generated from a specific project, which is riskier, and consequently pay a higher interest rate. The interest, which can be fixed or variable, is exempt from federal income tax and usually subject to a reduced local tax rate, which results in a lower yield. However, a municipal bond paying 6% interest may actually be a better investment than a taxable bond paying interest at 8% if you are in, say, the 28% tax bracket.

The federal government is also in the bond business, issuing a variety of bonds through the U.S. Treasury and other federal agencies. Interest on all treasury and some agency bonds is exempt from state and local taxes. Bonds issued directly by the federal government, which includes all the different types of treasury bonds as well as U.S. Savings Bonds, are the safest bond investments you can make. Federal agency bonds are the next-safest available bond investments. One type of federal bond, called Treasury Inflation-Protected Securities (TIPS), has a feature whereby the principal is adjusted by changes in the Consumer Price Index. If inflation occurs, the interest payment increases. In this way, your investment is protected against increases in the overall cost of living. It is important to consult with your financial advisor to determine which type of bond is best for you.

Corporate Bonds: Bonds issued by private companies, called corporate bonds, come in two basic varieties: Secured and unsecured. Secured corporate bonds are backed by a lien on the assets of the issuer, while unsecured corporate bonds are backed by the issuer's general credit. Interest and capital gains from corporate bonds are taxed at regular federal, state, and local rates.

The bond market offers a couple of other interesting options that are worth discussing. Some corporate bonds can be purchased as convertible bonds, which allow the holder to convert bond shares to common stock shares at a fixed-ratio. However, convertible bonds offer a lower yield than comparable non-convertible bonds.

Zero-coupon bonds: Also worth investigating are zero-coupon bonds. Zero-coupon bonds pay the holder no interest until maturity (as opposed to conventional bonds that pay interest every six months), but generally sell at a significant discount from face value. However, even though interest is not paid until maturity, the holder is still liable for annual taxes on the "phantom" interest that accrues. At maturity, the investor receives one lump sum payment equal to the principal plus interest.

Zero-coupon bonds can be issued by the U.S. Treasury, municipalities, and corporations. Zero-coupon bonds issued by municipalities or the U.S. Treasury avoid some of the issues created by this "phantom" interest tax. Placing a zero-coupon bond in an IRA is another way to avoid the hassle of paying taxes on interest you haven't collected yet. This is a popular strategy for college savings plans (see Chapter 7 for details). One potential downside of a zero-coupon corporate bond is that you lose all accrued interest if it defaults before maturity.

Bond ratings: To help you determine what level of risk a particular bond investment offers, all bonds are rated on a safety scale that uses credit ratings issued by Moody's Investor Service and Standard & Poor's Corp. The best bond rating is AAA, and the lowest bond rating still eligible for commercial investment is BBB/Baa. Bonds rated below BBB/Baa are popularly known as "junk bonds," and offer high yields but also a higher risk of default. The prudent *Just Don't Lose the Money* investor will avoid junk bonds.

Bond defaults at the commercial grade level are rare, but even within this level, prices and yields will vary, with the highest-rated bonds fetching the highest prices and lowest yields, which is often a favorable tradeoff in return for security. Remember that bonds issued by the federal government are the most secure and that shorter-term bonds are safer than longer-term bonds. As always, consult a financial professional before making any kind of bond investment.

JUMPING INTO THE POOL

During the past 20 years, mutual funds have exploded in popularity. A mutual fund is a collective investment in which investors pool their money to buy stocks, bonds, and/or other types of investments. A professional fund manager takes charge of the money and decides what assets to purchase with it. The price of a mutual fund, called the Net Asset Value, is determined by totaling the sum of all assets in the fund and dividing it by the number of shares.

Mutual funds offer a number of advantages that have made them appealing to many investors. One of the biggest advantages is the easy access they provide to a diverse investment holding. A mutual fund consists of numerous shares of numerous companies. Purchasing these shares individually would be time-consuming and financially draining, with separate fees and commissions for each transaction. But with a mutual fund, owning a single share can give you an ownership stake in literally hundreds of companies.

In addition, mutual funds offer the advantage of professional management. Most individual investors are not stock market experts. Mutual fund managers are stock market experts (or at least they should be!). As mentioned earlier in the chapter when we discussed buying individual stocks, a mutual fund investor does give up a lot of control over what stocks to buy and sell and when to buy and sell them. But investing in a well-run mutual fund can definitely produce profits that make this tradeoff worth it.

Despite these advantages, mutual funds are hardly risk-free. One of the biggest things to watch out for in a mutual fund is fees and costs, many of which may not be readily apparent. The more a mutual fund trades (or "churns"), the more its investors incur broker fees and other transaction fees. Some mutual funds charge a fee, or "load" to join or leave. Watch out for these "front load" and "back load" funds. Paying a "load" means you are essentially starting off with a loss.

Furthermore, the professional management you enjoy with a mutual fund is not a free add-on. Mutual funds charge an expense ratio, a percentage of the fund's total assets used for administration, management, advertising, and all other operational expenses. In addition, there will be service fees and other miscellaneous investor expenses.

The intent of providing you with all this information is not to dissuade you from investing in a mutual fund. Quite the contrary. What we are aiming to do is to stress the importance of doing your homework before purchasing any mutual fund shares. Most mutual funds in the same class will typically offer the same performance. A lesser-known fund with a lower expense ratio and lower fee structure may perform just as well as a comparable "superstar" fund with high costs. Organizations such as Morningstar provide useful information and ratings for mutual funds.

In addition, a fund with lower fees and costs can actually underperform a fund with higher fees and costs but still offer investors a better yield after the difference in cost structure is taken into account. To maximize your potential return on investment, look for options such as index funds, which have a low churn rate and low expense ratio. Index funds typically track the major stock market indexes and are less risky. Sector funds focus investments in a particular area, such as high tech or energy, and are prone to greater price fluctuations and risk.

While most mutual funds are not inherently dishonest, they are also usually not anxious to immediately explain all the varied costs of investing with them. Don't be afraid to ask a salesperson to give you a precise explanation of all direct and indirect costs before investing in a fund. Also look at who is managing the fund, how long that person has been in the job, and who their predecessors were. High management turnover can be a red flag that a mutual fund has problems, even if its financials appear to be strong.

As always, Uncle Sam wants his share of the mutual fund pie. You also need to be highly aware of the tax implications your mutual fund investment may carry. Capital gains distributions from mutual funds are taxable. That means if you invest in a mutual fund shortly before a capital gains distribution is scheduled, you will be paying tax on your investment almost immediately.

Also bear in mind that any mutual fund transaction which produces a profit is subject to capital gains tax, even if the value of the fund as a whole drops. This is another reason to seek funds with low churn.

Just Don't Lose the Money Tip
Diversify Your Variable Return Investments

The chart to the right shows why you should include at least some variable return investments, such as mutual funds, in your portfolio. Suppose you invested $100,000 in a tax-deferred account starting in 1977. If you put the money in a CD paying 4%, you would have about $311,000 by 2007 with little volatility.

However, if you put the same $100,000 in an index fund that tracks the S&P 500, you would have nearly $1.5 million! Yes, there were some ups and downs, but overall you would have earned five times as much money.

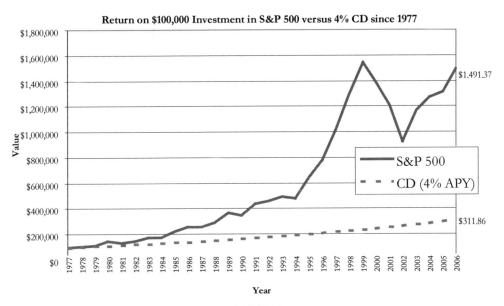

Return on $100,000 Investment in S&P 500 versus 4% CD since 1977

EXCHANGE TRADED FUNDS (ETFs)

Another category of pooled investments is known as Exchange Traded Funds, or ETFs. Put simply, ETFs are open-ended mutual funds that continually trade shares on the stock market. Rather than relying on a manager to select different investments that will maximize returns, ETF returns are linked to the performance of an index. This can be an established stock market index such as the S&P 500, as well as a specific market sector or commodity, or a proprietary index. For example, a well-known ETF, called SPDR (pronounced "spider"), is based on the S&P 500 index. Unlike mutual funds, ETFs do not necessarily trade at the same value as the investments they make up, and may trade at a small discount or premium depending on market demand.

ETFs can offer a number of expense and tax advantages over other pooled investments, such as traditional mutual funds. Institutional investors cover the initial costs of creating the ETF portfolio. In addition, ETFs typically feature lower expense ratios than mutual funds. Actively managed mutual funds generally charge 0.75-2% in annual fees, where ETFs generally charge in the range of 0.1-0.25% per year. This difference in annual fees can add up over a 20- or 30-year time horizon. ETFs may also provide a tax advantage over mutual funds. ETF shareholders usually only have to pay capital gains tax when they sell their shares for a profit, as opposed to paying capital gains tax on mutual fund share distributions. One potential drawback to ETFs is that since their shares are traded on the stock market, every ETF trade incurs commission costs. Most brokers charge commissions when investing in ETFs like any other stock. With small investments of money or frequent contributions, these commissions may erode your investment.

ETFs can serve as a worthy vehicle to invest your money and protect it from high-expense ratios and some capital gains taxes. Like mutual funds, investing in broad and diversified ETFs is much safer than investing in narrow ones. As always, you should consult with a qualified financial advisor to see if an ETF investment meets your particular needs before making any investments.

VARIABLE: THE OTHER ANNUITY

In the previous chapter, we discussed the value that fixed annuities can bring to your investment portfolio. Now it's time to look at variable annuities and the value they can bring to your investment portfolio if properly utilized.

Like a fixed annuity, a variable annuity is a contract with an insurance company that returns principal plus interest. Unlike a fixed annuity, which pays a preset interest rate, a variable annuity pays a flexible interest rate that is based on investments the holder makes with his or her premiums. Different variable annuities offer different investment options such as stocks, bonds, or mutual fund-type accounts. There is no yearly investment limit. Contributions cannot be deducted from income tax, but money inside a variable annuity grows tax-deferred until it is distributed or withdrawn, when it is taxed as ordinary income.

While the potential return for a variable annuity is greater than that of a fixed annuity, there is also a corresponding risk of losing money that a fixed annuity does not present. For an additional fee, variable annuities offer some options to reduce risk. One option guarantees a minimum income level in the event of a stock market decline. Also, some variable annuities offer principal protection features that guarantee you will get your initial investment back. In addition, variable annuities avoid probate and provide a variety of death benefit options.

Variable annuities often have an expense ratio as high as two percent, which is double that of a typical mutual fund. They also usually carry high surrender charges and other penalties. If you decide to invest in a variable annuity, carefully research all the angles and talk to a financial professional with variable annuity experience. While variable annuities can be useful investment vehicles, we do advise using caution and gathering sufficient information before making any variable annuity purchase.

A Quick Review

1 While purchasing individual stocks offers the best historical long-term return on investment, in the short-term it is a tricky proposition. The risks can be high, but the returns can also be high and there are a number of tax advantages. If you do purchase individual stock, perform careful research and only dedicate a small portion of your portfolio to this investment. Favor established blue-chip stocks that are expensive but stable over untested "hot" stocks that can gain and lose value unpredictably.

2 Bonds are a safer investment than stocks that offer a fixed interest rate. Bond values typically rise as stock values fall, making bonds a good hedge against stock-related investments. While bond interest is usually fixed, the value of bonds fluctuates on the secondary marketplace in reaction to the rise and fall of interest rates. The safest bonds are bonds issued by the federal, state, or local government, and any bonds with a credit rating below BBB/Baa are considered "junk" bonds and should be avoided.

3 Mutual funds offer a convenient way to diversify your stock holdings and spread out your investment risk. They also offer professional management. However, many mutual funds also contain hidden fees and may present certain tax disadvantages.

Just Don't Lose the Money Tip

Asset Allocation — A Little of This, A Little of That

As with fixed-return investments, you don't want to solely rely on one type of variable return investment to populate the variable return portion of your retirement portfolio. Especially considering the inherent risk associated with variable return investments, you want to spread your investments out.

Put your money in multiple mutual funds whose investment strategies don't overlap, as well as into some individual blue-chip stocks, AAA-rated bonds, and possibly a fixed annuity (preferably one with some minimum income guarantees). The more you diversify and spread the risk, the more you ensure that you won't lose the money!

Once the Paychecks Stop
Tax-Deferred Retirement Plans

It's great to have a job that you like. All day, everyday, you get up enjoying going to work and every two weeks you get a paycheck. Getting paid for something you like to do is a bonus. Sounds like a dream! Well, it can be. Retirement should be like that – getting up everyday, enjoying it, AND getting a paycheck to do it! Retirement planning MUST include a distribution plan with a strategy that delivers that paycheck every month.

Retirement is often referred to as "the golden years," a time when you can sit back, relax, and reflect on your career achievements. Golf, tennis, vacations, lots of birthday and Christmas presents for your adoring grandkids—that's what retirement is all about.

Is all of this attainable? Yes. Is it guaranteed? Hardly. As mentioned in Chapter 1, many financial experts now estimate that it will take 75 to 80 percent of your pre-retirement salary to maintain a comfortable post-retirement lifestyle. We say 90 percent. And "comfortable" doesn't necessarily mean three rounds of golf a week and a two-week cruise every summer. Comfortable means you have no major worries about where your next meal is coming from or if you'll still have roof over your head next month.

By now, the shortfalls of Social Security are clear to pretty much everyone. Living on Social Security income alone will most likely relegate you to a poverty-level lifestyle, and for those retirees or near-retirees who expect to live another 20, 30, or 40 years, Social Security may not even exist in its current form for that long.

Fortunately, there are a number of retirement planning options that allow you to put aside a portion of your paycheck while you're working and have that money either grow tax-deferred or be tax-free once you collect it. These options may allow you to take distributions in installments or in a lump sum. Most have rules restricting or penalizing you from withdrawing any money before a set age.

The most important thing to keep in mind about creating a retirement plan is that if you don't have one, you will most likely lose whatever money you have saved in other investments as you desperately try to fill the large financial gaps left by your monthly Social Security check. Some tax-advantaged retirement plan options are provided by your employer, some you can create on your own, but the savvy *Just Don't Lose the Money* investor will set one up and start contributing to it long before the "golden years" arrive. We will begin our in-depth discussion of retirement planning by looking at some of the common plans that employers provide.

THE GOOD OLD-FASHIONED PENSION

Once the most common retirement plan offered by public and private American employers, the pension has gradually lost favor in the private sector. Simply put, a pension is a guaranteed lifetime annuity for the employee. A pension is a defined benefit plan, meaning that the employee receives a set amount of money for his or her lifetime. The exact benefit amount is usually tied to how many years the employee spent with the company or how much salary they earned.

The major advantage of pensions is that employees make no contributions; the employer entirely finances the pension. This is the main reason that private employers have shied away from offering pensions and are instead turning toward defined contribution plans such as the 401(k) (we will explain all about defined contribution plans shortly).

Pensions do not entirely work toward the advantage of the employee, however. They do not travel with the employee upon a change of jobs, and if an employee leaves a company before their pension fully vests (a process that generally takes at least five years), they will collect nothing. This puts people who may have frequently changed jobs during their career at a serious disadvantage. Also, since many pensions are fixed and do not provide a cost-of-living increase, they may become far less valuable over time as inflation rises.

You Can Take It with You

Since the 1980s, private sector employers have been migrating away from defined benefit plans to defined contribution plans. Unlike defined benefit plans, defined contribution plans offer no set payment amount, but base their distributions on the investment performance of individual accounts that are set up for each individual employee.

While the employer may limit the types of investments an account-holder can make, usually the employee has at least some control over where money paid into their individual account goes, and participation is always voluntary.

The most common type of defined contribution plan offered by U.S. employers is the 401(k). Money that goes into a 401(k) is usually invested in stocks, bonds, or mutual funds. Some companies limit 401(k) investments to corporate stock.

Unlike pensions, the bulk of the responsibility for contributing to a 401(k) falls on the shoulders of the employee. Contributions are made in pretax dollars that are typically withdrawn directly from the employee's paycheck. Employers also have the option of matching a certain percentage of employee 401(k) contributions. Total 401(k) contributions by employees and employers are capped by IRS limits that usually change each year. For 2007, the contribution limit for a 401(k) participant was $15,500.

Another major differentiator between 401(k)s and pensions is that you can take a 401(k) with you from job to job, as long as your new employer also participates in a 401(k) program. You also have the option, when you change jobs to roll over the 401(k) into an Individual Retirement Account (IRA). IRAs are discussed later in this chapter. This portability is one of the 401(k)'s biggest advantages, especially in an era where job stability is no longer the norm.

Assets in a 401(k) grow tax free and are not subject to income tax until you begin to withdraw the money. So the 401(k) is a great way to build up tax-deferred savings for retirement. Keep in mind that any withdrawals made from a 401(k) before you reach age 59 ½ are subject to a 10 percent penalty in addition to income tax. Upon retirement, you will receive all the principal, earnings, and interest built up in your 401(k) as a lump sum.

To delay taxes further and stretch out your distribution period, you can roll that lump sum over into an IRA. To maximize your tax advantage, have your employer perform a direct trustee-to-trustee transfer of your 401(k) funds to an IRA. Otherwise, if the money enters your hands at any time during the transfer, 20 percent of the roll-over will be withheld until the following year's income taxes are due.

Pre-tax vs. After-tax Contributions

A trade-off to consider and discuss with your financial advisor is whether to make pre-tax or after-tax contributions to a 401(k) or IRA. After you retire, when you withdraw pre-tax contributions they are taxed as ordinary income, which is usually a higher tax rate than other investments such as capital gains and dividends. The benefit, however, is that you get to invest more money because you do not have to pay the tax right away. You can have the money you would have paid in taxes work for you right away until it is time to withdraw it. At that point, you will have to pay the tax.

With after-tax contributions, which are usually found in Roth type plans, you pay the tax on your contributions up front, but you will be able to withdraw the money tax-free when you retire. In short, paying a little bit of tax upfront could save you a lot down the road. It is important to consider the pros and cons of each approach with your financial advisor.

There are a couple of other varieties of the 401(k) besides the traditional one. The Roth 401(k) or Roth K takes employee contributions in after-tax dollars, and employees can contribute up to $15,000 per year ($20,000 if you are over 50 years old). Unlike the Roth IRA (covered later in this chapter), a Roth 401(k) has no annual income limits. Employer contributions are made in pretax dollars and taxed upon distribution, while any money invested by the employee is distributed tax-free. Currently the Roth 401(k) is set to lapse in 2010, but considering its current popularity, there is a strong chance it will become a permanent feature of the retirement planning landscape.

In a SIMPLE 401(k) (Savings Incentive Match Plan for Employees), the employer defines a percentage of each employee's pay that can be contributed (up to a federal maximum percentage). The employee decides where to invest the money and the employer must match at least three percent of contributed pay or two percent of all employee's pay (including the pay of non-participating employees). Money is invested in pretax dollars and grows tax-deferred.

Also worth mentioning are the 403(b) plan and 457 plan. The 403(b) is essentially a 401(k) plan designed for public educators, employees of non-profit organizations, and self-employed ministers. It is taxed identically to a 401(k). The 457 is essentially a 401(k) for governmental and certain non-governmental employees. It is also taxed identically to a 401(k), except there is no extra penalty for withdrawals made before age 59 ½.

With careful investing, any variety of 401(k) plan is an ideal retirement planning vehicle for a *Just Don't Lose the Money* investor. Since you're investing for retirement, your goal should be preservation of principal over earning interest, so look for secure investments with steady earnings. Usually you will have a variety of investment options ranging from mutual funds, bond funds, and company stock. One mistake employees should avoid is putting too much of their 401(k) assets in their company's stock. According to the NASD (National Association of Securities Dealers), 16% of employees over the age of 60 held more than 80% of their 401(k) savings in company stock. After the collapse of companies such as Enron, whose stock declined 99% in one year, the problem of putting all of your eggs in your company's basket should be obvious. Some 401(k) plans are more restrictive than others, but by consulting with a financial professional you should be able to design a 401(k) investment strategy that will suit your post-retirement needs.

401(k) plans that offer employer matching are especially advantageous, as they offer the extremely rare opportunity to make "free" money. If possible, always contribute enough of your pretax salary to your 401(k) to obtain the highest percentage of employer matching funds.

BE YOUR OWN BOSS

More Americans than ever are self-employed. Self-employment offers independence, freedom, and the ability to be responsible to nobody but yourself (and hopefully your customers and/or clients, of course!)—all the things about life that we individually-minded Americans cherish. However, part of your responsibility to yourself is the responsibility to provide a retirement plan.

That's where the Keogh plan comes in. The Keogh is basically a pension plan designed for self-employed people. Contributions are deductible from your taxable income. There are many different kinds of Keogh plans; you can set one up to work as either a defined benefit plan or as a defined contribution plan. The IRS sets limits on maximum annual contributions. Interest and earnings grow tax-deferred, with a penalty on withdrawals before age 59 ½.

You can open a Keogh plan even if you work for somebody else but also have your own side business. Anyone whose sole means of income comes from self-employment should definitely consult with a financial professional about opening a Keogh plan. One important factor to keep in mind is that if you are your own boss but also have employees, you must make any Keogh plan you open available to all your full-time employees.

OTHER EMPLOYER-SPONSORED RETIREMENT PLANS

You may find yourself working for a company that provides a number of additional retirement plans. These include the Simplified Employee Pension (SEP), which is a non-portable, tax-deferred vehicle that features flexible employee contributions but no employer matching, as well as Employee Stock Ownership (ESOP), which allows you to purchase or receive tax-deferred shares of corporate stock.

There is also profit-sharing, which may be offered as taxable cash distributions or as a tax-deferred lump sum at the end of your employment, and many more additional options than we cannot list in detail here. Generally speaking, if your employer offers a retirement plan, you should probably participate. This does not exclude you from investing in some of your own retirement plans, such as an IRA or annuity (see below), but employer-sponsored plans do offer a number of advantages.

For example, a corporate plan offers you federal-level creditor protection, as opposed to state-level creditor protection for a private plan. Qualified corporate plans allow you to borrow funds or use them to purchase life insurance. You can delay mandatory distribution from a corporate plan if you're still working at age 70 ½, and if you leave a job after age 55 but before age 59 ½, you can remove funds without paying any early withdrawal penalty.

All that said, a prudent investor will set up some kind of private retirement account in addition to participating in a corporate retirement plan. Besides offering you complete control, a private account allows you to extend the tax-advantage status of funds distributed from a corporate plan and is also easier to bequeath to your heirs. Let's take a run through some of the most popular of these investment vehicles.

THANK YOU, MISTER COHEN

The Individual Retirement Account (IRA) is one of the primary personal retirement planning vehicles available today. Legend has it that when Congress was creating the IRA in 1974, they were inspired by the first name of Ira Cohen, an actuary helping them develop the program, in determining an acronym to describe it. Whether this is true or not, one fact which cannot be argued is that IRAs have helped millions of Americans build tax-advantaged shelters for their retirement savings.

A traditional IRA is a tax-deferred account that allows an individual to contribute up to $4,000 per year (as of 2007, but the limit will increase to $5,000 in 2008). Interest and earnings on contributions grow tax-free until they are withdrawn or distributed, at which point they are taxed as regular income. Money within an IRA can be invested in a variety of ways, although IRAs offered by different institutions may have different rules and restrictions regarding investment. Mutual funds are a popular investment option for IRAs.

For the most part, any money you withdraw from a traditional IRA before the age of 59 ½ will be subject to a 10 percent penalty in addition to whatever taxes are owed. There are certain exceptions to this penalty, such as if the money is withdrawn to pay for certain educational expenses (see Chapter 7 for more details) or is used for first-time home building expenses.

As mentioned earlier in this chapter, distributions from a 401(k) can be rolled over to an IRA to continue their tax-deferred growth, though as explained the best method for doing this is a direct trustee-to-trustee transfer. However, money cannot sit and grow tax-deferred in a traditional IRA forever.

Each traditional IRA carries a Required Beginning Date (RBD) for its owner to start taking distributions. The RBD is April 1 of the year following the year you turn 70 ½. For each following year, the RBD is December 31. Penalties for missing your RBD can run as high as 50 percent, so be sure to mark your calendar!

As a side note to the RBD, if you wait until the year following the year you turn 70 ½ to take your first required mandatory distribution (RMD), you will have to take your second distribution by December 31 of that year. Therefore, it is better to take the first RMD the same year you turn 70 ½ to spread out the tax hit. After all, that money you withdraw could still be sitting inside your IRA, earning tax-deferred interest!

There are a variety of IRA options available, but outside of the traditional IRA the most noteworthy is the Roth IRA. Named for Senator William Roth (this is an established fact, unlike the story about our friend Ira Cohen), Congress created the Roth IRA in 1998 to provide an alternate means of saving money for retirement.

The most significant difference between a Roth IRA and a traditional IRA is that investments made in a Roth IRA use after-tax dollars. That is, you pay income tax on the money you contribute to your Roth IRA. The savings come when you withdraw the principal and interest years later, tax-free. That's right, because you've already paid tax on the money going in, you don't have pay any tax on it coming out.

You must hold a Roth IRA account for five years before taking any distributions and the same 10 percent penalty applies to withdrawals taken before age 59 ½ (with the same exceptions). Original principal can be withdrawn at any time. And unlike a traditional IRA, the

Roth IRA has no RBD or RMD associated with it. You can contribute money past age 70 ½, unlike a traditional IRA, and in theory never have to withdraw a dime!

Many financial experts promote the Roth IRA over the traditional IRA, citing the huge post-retirement tax break and looser restrictions on distributions and withdrawals. However, there is no objective answer about whether a traditional or Roth IRA is the "better" choice. Consult a financial professional to see which option best suits your individual retirement planning needs.

One thing which is undisputable is the immense value either type of IRA holds for the *Just Don't Lose the Money* investor. The IRA is one of the best tax-advantaged shelters in which you can invest. You save a bundle on taxes either going in or coming out, and by making prudent investments inside the IRA, you can build up quite a nice asset reserve for your post-retirement years.

As mentioned earlier, IRAs provide a great option to continue the tax-deferred growth of corporate retirement plans and to stretch out lump-sum distributions. IRAs are also relatively easy to pass on to your beneficiaries (see Chapter 11 for more details). We all like to grumble about some of the ridiculous decisions Congress has made over the years, but creating the IRA was one decision where Congress can honestly say it earned the salary paid by our hard-earned tax dollars.

Time to Catch-up

In an effort to increase retirement savings, Congress passed "catch-up" provisions that allow workers age 50 and over to increase their annual retirement plan contributions. For employer accounts, including 401(k)s, 403(b)s, and 457 plans, the "catch-up" provisions allow for additional contributions of up to $5,000 per year. For individual accounts (IRAs), you can contribute an additional $1,000 per year if you are 50 or over.

DID WE MENTION ANNUITIES?

In the previous chapter, we discussed how fixed annuities, and to a lesser extent variable annuities, offer a smart investment for *Just Don't Lose the Money* investors. Annuities are also a viable alternative (or complement) to IRAs for private retirement planning. Annuities can be used to replace the traditional pension plan (which, as noted above, many companies are discontinuing) since they provide a consistent stream of income. We don't need to rehash the details of how annuities work, but we strongly advise that any annuity specifically set aside to provide income or security for your post-retirement years be of the fixed or fixed-index variety. However, variable annuities with guaranteed minimum income levels or principal protection options are also viable alternatives to insure the happiness and comfort of your "golden years."

Immediate-income annuities are a useful option for retirees looking to create a safe, stable stream of income similar to a traditional retirement plan. With an immediate-income annuity, you give an insurance company a sum of money in exchange for the promise to send you regular income payments for the rest of your life or for a period of years. The income payments begin right away, and there is no deferral or waiting period. Immediate annuities can be an appropriate and simple way to invest some of your assets after you have retired.

Two problems with immediate annuities are that you give up your principal to create income, and once you start the income stream you do not have the option to stop it. In order to overcome these objections, insurance companies (all annuities are issued by insurance companies) have created a new type of immediate annuity. This new lifetime income product is typically a fixed annuity where the interest credited is either linked to some type of index or earns bank CD-like rates. There is also a guaranteed minimum return of 4 or 5 percent. The benefit of this newer type of annuity is that after one year you can create a minimum guaranteed lifetime income without giving up your principal. In addition, you can, if you choose, stop the yearly payout.

This type of flexibility helps when considering asset diversification choices. Each year you can choose where to take income from—an equity mutual fund that has done well or if it is a down year in the market, your guaranteed minimum lifetime income account.

MANAGING INCOME FROM YOUR TAX-DEFERRED RETIREMENT PLANS AFTER YOU RETIRE

Setting up, regularly contributing to, and carefully monitoring the investments of your tax-deferred retirement plans is half the battle. The other half occurs when you take distributions. No matter how intelligently you manage your money while it's inside a tax-deferred investment vehicle, if you make a dumb mistake by withdrawing it, all your effort and care will be wasted. The taxman will take too large a bite or you will simply take too much out at one time and not leave enough for your future needs. The key is making sure that you have enough income during your retirement years.

How do you manage income from a tax-deferred retirement plan? Here are six quick tips to help you keep the money once it leaves tax-advantaged status and enters your hands:

Just Don't Lose the Money Tip

Diversify Your Retirement Investments

In addition to diversifying your fixed and variable return investments, you should also diversify your tax-advantaged investments that you are counting on to provide income in your post-retirement years. Corporate plans often have their drawbacks, such as limited investment options or lump sum distributions, and if the company you worked for goes bankrupt or has other problems during your retirement years, it could jeopardize your investment.

Always buffer any corporate retirement plan with private plans such as IRAs or annuities. In addition to providing extra security, they also can provide a great place to put distributions from corporate plans to continue tax-advantaged growth!

1. Draw down your portfolio according to your life expectancy. The IRS provides life expectancy tables for single and married people, based on your current age. While trying to statistically determine how many years you have left on this earth may seem a little morbid, it is also a prudent way to help determine how much of your savings you can withdraw in any one year and still leave enough money behind to last for the remainder of your life. If the IRS tables say you have 20 years left, you can withdraw up to 1/20th (or five percent) of your savings in that year without leaving yourself short in the future. In the following year you would withdraw 1/19th and so on. One downside of this approach is if your investments declined in a particular year, you would have to sell shares in a down market.

2. Draw down your portfolio like a non-profit. Non-profit organizations calculate a weighted average five-year balance for their investment portfolios and then withdraw a fixed percentage of that average each year. This helps protect against year-to-year fluctuations and aberrations in portfolio performance. You can determine the same five-year balance for your own investment portfolio and withdraw accordingly. For example, you could take five percent per year of a five-year average account balance. Using a five-year weighted average should help reduce swings in withdrawals due to market fluctuations.

3. Provide for short-term income needs with a money market deposit account. As described in Chapter 2, a money market deposit account (MMDA) is a (sometimes) higher-interest, high-minimum-balance deposit account that is designed for savings, but allows the holder limited capability to write checks and perform other transfers. You can determine your short-term financial needs (up to three years) and place enough money in an MMDA to cover them. That way you can take distributions from the MMDA without having to worry about fluctuations in the market. During years when the market goes up, you can then replenish the MMDA with dividends and distributions from the rest of your portfolio.

4. Take taxable distributions from your IRA. Legally, you don't have to start taking IRA distributions till age 70 ½, but there is also nothing preventing you from taking them starting at age 59 ½ while paying nothing but regular income tax. By taking taxable distributions before mandatory distributions kick in, up to the point they fill the 15 percent income tax bracket, you can save money on taxes later in life by reducing minimum distribution requirements.

5. Segregate the necessities from the luxuries. Some money you have to spend, some money you want to spend. There's a big difference, and investment needs for each kind of money are also different. Any money earmarked for basic, non-discretionary spending can be put aside in safe investments such as bonds or fixed annuities, while money earmarked for the finer things in life can be invested in more growth-oriented instruments. This ensures you can pay for the necessities while also taking acceptable risk with the money you have left over.

6. Pension Annuity – Another option is to purchase a guaranteed lifetime income annuity that provides an income stream similar to a traditional pension. These annuities provide a guaranteed minimum return or 4 or 5 percent without giving up your principal. In addition, you can start or stop your income at any time. This feature gives you flexibility to choose where to take income from in any given year—for example, you can draw from an equity mutual fund that has done well or from your guaranteed annuity if the stock market is having a bad year.

And of course, you should always follow the simple, old-fashioned rules of prudent investing. This means watching what you spend, diversifying your investment portfolio, avoiding any investment that offers high growth at high risk, focusing on keeping what you have, actively seeking ways to avoid or minimize taxes, and obtaining the proper insurance to cover you in the event of catastrophe. By following all these steps, you can help ensure that your money outlives you, rather than you outliving your money!

Peace of Mind for a Non-Working Spouse

In many instances, a non-working spouse will not have his or her own retirement account. For peace of mind, it is good idea to set up a retirement account for the non-working spouse. An annuity for a non-working spouse is a good way to equalize a couple's tax-deferred retirement accounts. For example, if the working spouse has $200,000 in an IRA, he could set up a retirement account for his non-working spouse (assuming the spouse is younger than 59 ½). He could put half of the $200,000 into an annuity for his non-working spouse which would provide lifetime income and peace of mind.

A QUICK REVIEW

1 You will need up to 90 percent of your pre-retirement income to sustain the lifestyle to which you are accustomed in your post-retirement years. Social Security alone is not a viable means to provide this type of financial security. You must start saving for your retirement as soon as possible, through employer-sponsored and/or private tax-advantaged retirement plans.

2 The most common tax-advantaged retirement plan offered by private employers today is the 401(k). A 401(k) is a defined contribution plan that offers no set distribution amount, but bases its distributions on the performance of individual accounts that are set up for each individual employee. Usually the individual employee has at least some say into how their 401(k) money is invested, and employers may match a certain percentage of employee contributions. Money grows tax-deferred until the employee retires, when it is distributed as a taxable lump sum or rolled over into an IRA.

3 An Individual Retirement Account (IRA) is a private investment account that allows an individual to invest up to $5,000 a year (as of 2008) with taxes on principal and interest deferred until distribution. You can also contribute to an IRA on behalf of a non-working spouse up to $4,000 per year. Withdrawals before age 59 ½ are penalized, with certain exceptions. The Roth IRA is an alternative mechanism that allows an individual to invest after-tax dollars with tax-free distribution. IRAs are an excellent retirement savings option and also can provide a shelter for distributions from 401(k) plans. In addition, fixed or fixed-index annuities offer a solid option for private retirement savings.

4 The right distribution plan should be explored well in advance of retirement.

5 Set up a retirement plan for non-working spouse.

Home Sweet Home
Personal Real Estate

The American Dream: *owning your own home and a good night's sleep. Building up equity in your home means you own it without a mortgage. I'm a no-debt guy. (In some cases there might be tax advantages to having a mortgage. Like I say, I'm an old-fashioned guy and I don't like debt.) Having no debt on your home brings certain benefits. You need less income to live on, you can always use the equity in your home to raise money, and most importantly, there's nothing better than a good night's sleep. No debt certainly makes me sleep better!*

For many Americans, owning a home is a symbol of "making it." There is a sense of security and well-being that only home ownership can provide. You have to live somewhere. Beyond whatever status and psychological comforts owning a home provides, home ownership also offers an excellent tax shelter and equity that can be tapped for personal use. Another benefit of home ownership is the homestead exemption, which in Massachusetts protects up to $500,000 in home equity from attachment by creditors.

Nonetheless, owning a home in your later years carries a number of pros and cons that need to be carefully examined before determining whether you should hold, buy, or sell a home. While home ownership typically implies a house, there are also some advantages to owning either a condominium or a co-op. In this chapter we will review how you can assess the likelihood that owning a home will help you ensure that you just don't lose the money.

For many years, conventional wisdom dictated that purchasing a home was the smartest long-term investment you could make. In the long-term, property values tend to go up, although that does not guard against the periodic slumps that are an inevitable feature of the real estate market. And as mentioned above, you build equity with your monthly mortgage payments that can serve as a line of personal credit or collateral for a loan.

However, in recent years some real estate and financial experts have begun challenging the conventional wisdom about home ownership. They argue that the actual monetary return on a home investment is low compared to investing the same amount of money in an alternative investment vehicle, such as the stock market.

They also argue that home equity is not the most efficient means of procuring personal credit or loans. And home ownership does require what usually amounts to substantial spending on property tax, maintenance, upkeep and improvements, insurance, and mortgage loan interest.

It would take an entire separate book to fully analyze the debate over the basic merits of home ownership, and in the end there would be no definitive resolution. Our opinion is that a home can represent a sound investment. We will concentrate on how to determine if it's an investment that makes sense for your particular situation.

Who Owns Your Home?

The answer to this question may seem ridiculously easy at first glance. The odds are that you do, or your spouse does, or perhaps you and your spouse own it jointly. Perhaps the name of a child or other beneficiary is also on the deed, or the ownership has been placed in a trust, to make inheritance easier and/or to protect your assets in the event you need long-term nursing home care (see Chapters 10 and 11 for details).

But before you answer, think about this: Do you have a mortgage, or perhaps even two mortgages? Then a bank or other financial institution owns a piece of your home, possibly a substantial piece. Also, if you have secured a loan through home equity, then there is a most likely a lien on your property ensuring that any proceeds from sale or liquidation of the home will first be used to pay off that loan before you see a dime. Liens can also result from unpaid back property taxes or other unresolved debts.

If you can honestly say you own your home outright, you have eliminated a significant portion of the expenses that can be associated with owning a home. Of course this still leaves taxes and maintenance-related costs, and both of those costs usually go up as a home ages. Make sure you take all costs and ownership/creditor issues into account when you look at potentially purchasing or selling a home.

SHOULD I PAY MY MORTGAGE EARLY?

Assuming you own a home and carry at least one mortgage on it, you may be tempted to pay off the mortgage early. Some mortgages feature an early payment penalty, but many allow you to pay off the remaining principal and interest at any time. This can allow you to save a substantial amount of money in the long run, since you will be paying interest for a shorter period of time.

However, there are several other factors to consider. One is the mortgage interest deduction you will lose on your annual federal income tax return. Depending on your individual tax situation, this may result in a significantly higher tax bill. But don't always let the tax tail wag the dog.

Another item to think about is that the same money you use to pay your mortgage off early could be invested some other way at potentially higher profit. If you are paying 6.5 percent interest on your mortgage, the extra money you use to pay it off early will save you 6.5 percent/year over the remaining term of your mortgage. You may be able to locate an investment vehicle that will offer a higher return for the same period of years. Also, the value of your fixed mortgage payment decreases over time due to inflation. A $1,400/month

Just Don't Lose the Money Tip

Mortgage Payment Frequency

Depending on your cash flow, if you make your current mortgage payments every two weeks instead of every month, you can take 7 or 8 years off the life of a 30-year loan. You will also reduce the total interest by 20-35% depending on the interest rate.

Take, for example, a 30-year mortgage with 6.5% APR on a $200,000 principal:

	Monthly	Bi-Weekly
Individual Payment	$1,264.14	$632.07
Total Interest	$255,008.98	$194,430.48
Avg. Monthly Interest	$708.58	$538.70
Years of Repayment	30	23

payment in 2007 will actually cost you less five or ten years from now if your other income and investments increase in value due to appreciation and inflation.

Sometimes the determining factor on whether or not you pay off early is the "Sleep Factor": Does it make you sleep better at night knowing you will be debt free sooner? As always, consult with a financial professional before deciding whether or not to pay off a mortgage early.

ARE YOU HOUSE POOR?

When buying a home, there is a natural impulse to buy the nicest possible house you can afford. Resist it. "House poor" is the common term used for people who afford their home by putting virtually all of their savings into it. In this way you can build some impressive equity, but you will have no other significant assets to your name. This situation could lead to a "liquidity trap." If an emergency hits or if you just need cash to pay for a wedding, and you need to liquidate your main asset, you will have a hard time liquidating quickly and will likely get a poor or even negative return on your investment, with nothing else in your portfolio to balance the loss.

As a rule of thumb, try to keep total principal, interest, and insurance payments on your home to approximately a third or less of your net income. This keeps your home within your budgetary limits and leaves money available for other investments. On a less scientific note, you also may want to resist the urge to buy the "nicest house on the block." You are paying the maximum entry fee to get into a particular neighborhood and are improving your neighbors' resale value while they are not helping and may even be hurting yours.

REFINANCING A MORTGAGE/SECOND MORTGAGE/EQUITY CREDIT

Refinancing a mortgage simply means that you replace your existing first mortgage with a new first mortgage that has better payment terms, either in terms of interest rate or payment schedule. You can then use the money you are saving to pay off the balance of the existing mortgage, and maybe even make some profit in the process.

A second mortgage is an additional mortgage loan you take out, usually for a smaller amount and payable in a shorter period of time than your first mortgage. One of the most common types of second mortgage is the home equity line of credit. Your equity becomes collateral for a loan, and in turn you are able to write checks or make credit card purchases against the equity.

Before taking a home equity line of credit or any other second mortgage, keep in mind that the interest rate is typically higher than the rates offered for first mortgages. The interest rate will generally be one to three points above the prime rate, adjusted monthly up to a cap based on the initial interest rate. Interest paid on a second mortgage for $100,000 or less is tax-deductible.

These different methods of manipulating your mortgage can be financially beneficial, but only if they are put to use for a good cause, such as paying off a debt, freeing capital for an investment, or creating an educational fund. Never look to your mortgage or home equity to raise money for activities such as buying an automobile, financing a vacation, or even obtaining some spending money. You'll gain money in the short term but almost certainly lose it in the long term!

If you're genuinely having a hard time affording the basic necessities, you may want to consider selling your home and finding a cheaper living arrangement rather than saddling yourself with additional mortgage debt. As an added bonus, up to $250,000 in individual profits (or $500,000 in profits for a married couple) from a home sale are not subject to capital gains tax and therefore tax-free.

REVERSE MORTGAGES

In a reverse mortgage, a bank or other financial institution takes your house as collateral on a loan and then releases the equity to you, either in a lump sum or in installments. Unlike a traditional mortgage, in a reverse mortgage you receive payments rather than make them. However, the reverse mortgage issuer takes a lien on your home and has the principal and interest of the loan repaid when the home is sold or the owner dies or enters a nursing home. It allows you to get liquidity from your home but will impact your ability to pass the house on to your loved ones.

The money you receive from reverse mortgage payments is not directly taxable but may count as liquid assets depending on how you save or invest them, which can affect your eligibility for public programs such as Medicaid. A reverse mortgage must be the only mortgage you hold on your home, although you can pay off an existing mortgage with proceeds from a reverse mortgage. Also, a homeowner must be 62 or older to qualify for a reverse mortgage.

Exact costs of a reverse mortgage vary but are usually high. They typically have adjustable interest rates. Expert opinion seems split on reverse mortgages, but the general consensus seems to be that you

---

There is also the possibility of a private reverse mortgage. You borrow money from a friend or relative who might want your home when you pass away. They can lend with substantially less closing costs and a fixed interest rate.

---

should proceed with caution. Before obtaining a reverse mortgage, you are required by federal law to undergo free credit counseling from a Department of Housing and Urban Development (HUD)-approved source, and we urge you to speak with a qualified financial professional in addition to receiving this free counseling.

Ultimately, reverse mortgages offer you access to the equity you have built up in your home, and they should be approached the same way you would approach opening a line of home equity credit. If you do decide to pursue a reverse mortgage, make sure it is for a worthy cause and not to simply free up some more cash. Remember our golden rule: Just don't lose the money!

OTHER HOUSING OPTIONS – CONDOS, CO-OPS AND APARTMENTS

Later in life, many people decide that it's time to sell their house and downsize to a smaller, more affordable living arrangement. There are many reasons to do so. With the kids grown up and gone, those empty bedrooms don't serve much purpose, and as you enter the fixed-income period of your life, all the aforementioned expenses of house ownership become an even more onerous burden. For example, property taxes have increased rapidly in recent years, so why pay tax on extra rooms that you do not need anymore?

We will examine three alternatives to living in a house that you own: living in a condo that you own, living in a co-op that you own, or renting some type of dwelling, which could be a house, condo, co-op, or apartment. All these alternatives offer advantages and disadvantages and may serve as a means to help you avoid losing the money.

YOURS, MINE, AND OURS

When you own a house, usually what you own is pretty cut and dried. You own the physical structure of the house plus the land it sits on and any other structures (such as garages and sheds) on the property. If something breaks, you are responsible for fixing it. Unless you live in a neighborhood with historic landmark rules or other local restrictions, you can modify the house or property as you wish within reason—major renovations or changes usually require approval from the jurisdiction in which you live and possibly your immediate neighbors.

In a condominium arrangement, things operate a little differently. You possess all the rights to your own housing unit (usually called a "condo"), and own a proportional share of joint interest in the land the condo development sits on and all common areas, such as parking lots, swimming pools, and yard space. Almost any type of dwelling can be made into a condo; townhouses and apartments are two popular choices. You can purchase a condo with a conventional government-backed mortgage.

Beware of Special Assessments

Condo owners are sometime hit with special assessments above and beyond the monthly maintenance fee. For example, suppose you owned a condo in a 30-unit building near the ocean and the exterior of the building had to be replaced for $1.8 million. Each condo owner would be assessed $60,000 as a "special assessment" to pay for the repairs. Because decisions are dictated by the condo association, you lose your own choice to make a repair or improvement and how much to spend.

A condominium development is controlled and operated by a condo association. The association sets and oversees the rules and regulations of the condo development and also collects monthly maintenance and management fees. As opposed to owning a house, when you own a condo, you are usually not responsible for repairs outside of your individual unit unless there is a special assessment. Your monthly fees help pay for a maintenance staff that is responsible for repairs and general upkeep of the common areas, as well as for maintaining the grounds and other similar tasks.

Usually a condo association will employ directors and managers to collect, track, and invest fees, and oversee day-to-day operations of the development. This association arrangement represents the biggest pros and cons of living in a condo. On the plus side, you don't have to worry about many of the maintenance and operational aspects of owning a house. You can sell or rent your condo at any time.

On the negative side, you pay what may be fairly hefty monthly fees for the privilege of letting someone else take care of it, you have to trust the association and its managers to invest and spend those fees wisely, and you also give up a lot of independence. Most condo associations have strict rules regarding how your condo can look and forbid any type of enlargement or other changes to your condo's structure.

Furthermore, many condo associations have rules restricting or banning pets and many restrict the age of people who can live in a development (which can turn into a plus for those with animal allergies or older folks happy to live in a 55-plus development!) If you decide to sell your condo, you will find that condos appreciate slower and depreciate quicker than houses, and have less of a resale market. In many parts of the country, such as Florida, condos have been overbuilt and there is currently a glut in the market.

One alternative method of joint housing ownership is the cooperative development, popularly known as a "co-op." In a co-op, residents own shares of stock in a company that owns the co-op development. Each resident is technically a tenant of the company who is entitled by their stock ownership to live in the co-op. Co-op purchases must be financed by a share loan, not a mortgage.

You pay monthly fees in a co-op development like you do in a condo development, but unlike a condo development, you can deduct your share of the co-op development's mortgage interest and taxes from your own tax payments. Co-op owners can rent or sell their units at any time.

If you find yourself "house poor" or are simply fed up with the high costs and efforts of owning a house, moving to a condo may be a good way to save money on housing expenses; money that could be reinvested elsewhere. There is no single answer as to whether owning a condo or co-op is a better way to hang onto your money than owning a house. Consult a financial expert before making such a major life decision.

To Own or Not to Own

Nobody ever said you have to own the place where you dwell. You always have the option to rent. You can rent a house, condo, co-op unit, or apartment for significantly less money than it would take to buy one. Like a condo or co-op, you are not responsible for repairs and maintenance, but unlike a condo or co-op, you don't have to pay a special fee to obtain maintenance services.

When you don't own your dwelling, property value becomes much less of a concern, and it's much easier to pull up stakes and move. You also don't have to directly pay any property taxes or mortgage, although these costs will be figured into your rent. Naturally, you lose the opportunity to deduct these expenses from your federal taxes, although some states offer a rent deduction.

Renting does offer some significant downside besides losing some tax deductions. Your living situation is far less secure, as your landlord may not renew your lease, or even give you 30 days' notice if you are a month-to-month tenant. Your rental payments build no equity, they represent money that goes directly into someone else's pocket and never benefits you again. And restrictions on things like making alterations to the property and pet ownership will usually be far stricter for a renter than they are even for a condo or co-op owner.

All that said, for some people renting is a good option. If you live on your own or in a large urban area, renting may make more sense than owning or buying. An additional rental option is to create a sales leaseback arrangement for your home with your child. This involves selling your home to your child with the provision of a lease that allows you to live there for the remainder of your life.

By financing the mortgage loan privately, you obtain the down payment and monthly mortgage payments while your child receives the monthly rent and the tax benefits of home ownership. This provides the additional benefit of protecting your assets in the event you need nursing home care (see Chapter 10 for more details).

Before entering any kind of rental agreement, particularly if you plan to sell your home as part of the plan, consult a financial professional. Renting can be a viable housing option, but if you get yourself stuck with high rent or other unfavorable lease conditions, you could find yourself losing the money.

A QUICK REVIEW

1 House ownership provides an excellent tax shelter, builds equity, gives protection from creditors, and provides personal security. However, it is also an expensive proposition that involves paying for a mortgage, property taxes, insurance, and maintenance and repairs. Carefully research the pros and cons of owning a house, particularly as you enter your retirement years, and also carefully research the pros and cons of other house-related decisions such as taking a second mortgage, opening a line of home equity credit, or paying off a mortgage early.

2 Condos and co-ops are alternative home ownership options that are generally cheaper to buy, and remove the burden of performing maintenance and repairs. They also involve paying monthly fees and generally restrict what you can do with your dwelling. Furthermore, they generally offer lower resale value than houses.

3 Renting a home may present a viable alternative to buying one. Renting is much cheaper than buying, and renters obtain free maintenance services from their landlords. In addition, renters do not directly pay any property taxes or mortgages. On the downside, renters do not build any equity with their rent payments and are in a less secure and independent living situation than homeowners. They also lose the tax breaks associated with paying property tax and mortgage interest.

Just Don't Lose the Money Tip
Avoid Probate

Probate is a legal proceeding conducted by a state court that oversees the distribution of your property after you die. It is time-consuming, can be costly, and also makes all the details of your personal and family finances available for the world to see. By placing your personal real estate assets in a trust, you can ensure that they directly pass to your beneficiaries without the hassle and cost of probate (see Chapter 11 for details about trusts).

Another option is the Life Estate, which allows you to retain the use of your home while directing the remainder to pass to someone else when you die without going through probate or paying estate recovery charges for nursing home care (see Chapter 11 for more details about Life Estates). This is only useful in states that limit their claims to property in your probate estate for repayment of Medicaid/nursing home costs (see Chapter 9 for details about Medicaid). Also keep in mind that creating a Life Estate may create gift-tax liabilities and that once you place property in a Life Estate, you cannot sell it without approval of the named beneficiaries or engage in "wasteful" use of the property (i.e., use that damages or devalues it).

A final option for avoiding probate with real estate is joint tenancy with right of survivorship. You can add your children or other loved ones to the deed as joint owners, and the property will pass without having to go through probate. Transfer of the property at death is automatic in this situation. However, any time you transfer ownership of real estate to a non-spouse, there are tax consequences you should be aware of. In addition, "just putting your child's name" on a deed may cause more problems if either the child predeceases you, gets sued, or gets divorced.

Be careful!

The Real Scoop on Investment Real Estate

Only the strong survive. Many people who invest in real estate are strong, not physically but financially. In order for investments in real estate to work for you, you must be strong. That is, having enough money to get you past the bad times. Speaking about strong, there is nothing better than strong family ties. Vacation homes that you use with growing children and grandchildren create those strong family ties that are invaluable. If you can afford a vacation home without stress, do it. The family benefits you will reap will make you rich.

There are many types of real estate investments you can make beyond purchasing your primary residence. You may want to buy a vacation home or timeshare as a place to relax and serve as a "home away from home," or rental property to earn income and obtain tax breaks as a landlord.

Real estate can be an excellent investment that will help you "not lose the money" as you enter your retirement years, but can also be a tricky investment to manage. In this chapter we will look at some of the different real estate investment options that exist and how to determine if they're the right place for you to put some of your hard-earned cash.

Home Away From Home – Is The Vacation Home Worth It?

A vacation home can be a chalet at a ski resort, a cottage on the beach, or a deluxe villa in some exclusive, secluded spot. You may spend a few days or several months a year there. The key is that it serves as a home away from home, a place where you can unwind and let go some of the cares of everyday life that consume you at your home that is home. But if it becomes a financial burden—it's just not worth it.

Speaking bluntly, purchasing a vacation home with the intent of primarily using it for personal enjoyment or the enjoyment of your family members is not the smartest financial move you can make, but given the right circumstances, it can add years of enjoyment to your life. Buying a vacation home often involves taking out a second mortgage or home equity line on your primary residence, which incurs additional debt. You can deduct the mortgage interest used to pay for a second home subject to certain limitations. The mortgage interest deduction applies for up to $1 million of principal on both your homes combined, which can help remove some of this second mortgage sting.

One way to reduce the financial burden posed by a vacation home (and possibly even turn it into a financial asset) is to rent it out when you're not using it. Obviously your ability to rent out a vacation home may be somewhat limited by seasonal factors, but you can rent it for up to 14 days a year without reporting the income or expenses. Considering what the weekly rental rates have risen to in many of the more desirable vacation spots, that could add up to many thousands of dollars of tax-free income.

Once you rent out a vacation home for more than 14 days in a given year, you are legally considered a landlord and must start reporting all rental income. If your personal use of the property (this extends to renting it out to family members or allowing anyone to stay there free or pay rent below market rates) totals more than 14 days a year or more than 10 percent of the days it is rented, the property is considered a personal residence for tax purposes. If your vacation home counts as a personal residence for two of the five years preceding a sale, you can sell it as a personal residence and get the tax break on the profits (see Chapter 5 for details).

Otherwise, your vacation home becomes a rental property for tax purposes. If you sell it while it is considered a rental property, you will owe full tax on all profits. However, you will also pick up a number of tax write-offs afforded to owners of rental properties (we will explain those shortly).

If you are considering purchasing a vacation home that will primarily serve as a recreational tool, look at it as a luxury. You can offset some of the cost through rentals, but unless its primary purpose will be as a source of rental income, don't expect to recoup your entire investment. We're not saying that buying a vacation home is a sure path to losing the money, just cautioning you that it should not be viewed as a mechanism to maintain or increase the return on whatever money you put into it.

Also, to determine the personal (non-monetary) value a vacation home will provide, honestly ask yourself how often you, your family, and/or friends will use it. If it will sit idle the bulk of the year, you may be better off renting a vacation home for just the time you would use it. To help maximize the possible return on your investment, select a home that offers good potential rental and resale value. If you think you may want to sell a vacation home in the near future, make sure you rack up a couple of years where it counts as a personal residence in order to enjoy the tax benefits of the sale.

Many times, paid off vacation property can help you "downsize" in your golden years. With two homes, your primary residence and vacation home, you can have a choice at retirement to sell your primary residence, thereby releasing the gain you made on that property. With that gain, you can purchase a smaller condo or "winter getaway" and

Just Don't Lose the Money Tip

A vacation home for personal use should not be a financial burden. Buy only what you can afford—you'll enjoy it more.

put more money in the bank.

We would like to make a brief side comment on timeshares. A time-share vacation unit is usually sold by the week, and you own the exclusive right to use the unit during your annual week(s). Your ownership of the unit will typically be reflected as tenancy in common with the other owners, meaning you can rent or sell your timeshare usage rights.

Timeshare owners must pay a variety of fees, such as maintenance, and can only finance their purchase via a loan from the timeshare developer or a personal loan. Resale value on timeshares tends to be extremely low. Even more so than a vacation home, a timeshare should be viewed strictly as a personal luxury with no real financial return on investment.

LIFE AS A LANDLORD (CAN BE HELL)

In this section we will look at property bought with the sole purpose of renting for a profit. A vacation home can fall into a nebulous area between personal and rental property, but here we are talking about property you buy with no intent of using for any personal purposes.

First, the good news: Landlords receive numerous tax breaks that other types of property owners do not. You can deduct items such as operating costs, mortgage insurance, real estate taxes, and expenses from rental income before it is taxed, even if the expenses exceed the rental income. However, if you use the property for both rental and personal purposes, you must divide your total expenses between the rental use and the personal use based on the number of days used for each purpose. You will not be able to deduct your rental expense in excess of your gross rental income in that case.

Another huge tax break offered to rental property owners is depreciation. You are allowed to deduct a certain percentage of the physical structure (though not the land it sits upon) each year, whether it actually shows any sign of deterioration or not. Depending on how much deterioration you are able to claim, you could potentially mitigate or even eliminate losses emanating from negative cash flow from a rental property. Depreciation allows you to deduct part of your cost for the property over a period of years, which for rental real estate is typically 27.5 years. For example, if you paid $275,000 for the rental property, you could deduct the $10,000 depreciation ($275,000 / 27.5 years) each year on your tax return for 27 years. Be aware that depreciation reduces your basis for figuring gain or loss on a later sale, and that it is a complex area of tax law so you should get professional advice when considering it.

Furthermore, rental losses themselves may be tax deductible. However, tax deductions from depreciation and rental loss may be limited, so be sure to consult a professional tax advisor before filing your return. Also, you can check out IRS Publication 527, Residential Rental Property (Including Rental of Vacation Homes), for more information.

Now for the not-so-good news: Profits on sales of rental properties are fully taxed as capital gains/personal income, without any of the tax breaks given to sellers of personal residences. Also, depreciating the property over a period of years has the effect of increasing your capital gains tax when you sell the property, since the depreciation deductions reduce your cost basis. And when you're the landlord, you become responsible for all reasonable repairs and upkeep. If one of your tenants calls to say their stove won't work (they usually call at night or on weekends), you bear the expense of fixing or replacing it.

For a handy person who only has a few tenants, this may not seem like such a large burden in terms of financial or time expense. But if you're not capable of personally making home repairs or performing routine maintenance, or if you own a large number of rental properties, you will need to hire someone else to resolve these issues.

The answer could be as simple as retaining the services of a part-time handyman or as complex as employing a full-time property manager and staff of maintenance personnel. These expenses are tax-deductible, but they can still add up quickly. And bear in mind that the rental market may often track the performance of the residential property market, with people more inclined to rent when homes are expensive to buy and less inclined to rent as homes become more affordable.

Rental property can be an excellent long-term investment, both in terms of the income they produce and their potential resale value. Some of the same arguments against buying a home can also apply against buying a rental property: Your money may produce a greater overall return if invested elsewhere.

Perform careful research before buying any investment property, especially if you will be "inheriting" existing tenants, and don't let the prospect of monthly rent coming in blind you to the significant maintenance and operational costs that usually come along with that rent. Don't forget to speak with a qualified real estate expert, as well. Being a landlord can be a great way of not losing the money, but it is hardly risk-free!

Just Don't Lose the Money Tip
Staying Strong

Rental real estate for the small investor can and does work over time. You must be strong in more than one way.

Be strong as a landlord—don't let a tenant get by without paying rent because you feel bad for them. This can bring down the whole project. On the other hand, don't neglect a tenant's needs. If something needs to be fixed or replaced—do it as quickly as possible. Be visible—show up at least once per month to check on your property.

Be strong financially—plan for a set back. Have enough in cash reserves to cover any financial disaster like not being able to rent a unit or problems with a heating system.

Remember, strong landlords survive—weak landlords perish.

OTHER INVESTMENT REAL ESTATE OPTIONS

There are other ways of investing in real estate, some of which do a better job of protecting your principal than others. We will briefly review the pros and cons of a few.

Real Estate Investment Trust (REIT) – An REIT works like a mutual fund. Investors pool their ownership of multiple real estate properties by purchasing shares. An Equity REIT invests in income-producing (rental or commercial) property, while a Mortgage REIT invests in long-term mortgage and short-term construction loans. A Hybrid REIT puts money in both types of real estate investments. REITs can be useful to help diversify your portfolio to include real estate investments without the headaches of actually managing and maintaining property.

REITs carry similar fees, expenses, and tax liabilities as mutual funds. However, investors can defer paying taxes on a portion of the dividends (considered return of capital) if at least 90 percent of the earnings go to REIT shareholders, and certain other conditions are met. REIT shares typically cost more than mutual fund shares but also typically offer higher dividends. Unlike mutual funds, the performance of REITs will usually closely mirror the performance of the general real estate market.

An REIT can be a smart investment that helps you keep the money (by not losing it, naturally), but they require careful research. You must check out the appraisals of the properties, dividend history, performance of the loans they invest in, and other pertinent issues. If you are not a real estate expert, REITs become an even trickier investment. Do your homework and consult a financial expert with real estate knowledge before purchasing any shares of an REIT.

Real Estate Limited Partnership – A Real Estate Limited Partnership is a group of investors who pool their money and directly invest in real estate holdings. The advice here is simple: Run in the other direction! These partnerships are complex and extremely risky for anyone who is not a professional real estate expert.

"Expert" doesn't mean someone who has invested in a lot of real estate; it means someone who has spent years in a full-time job in the real estate industry and knows all the ins and outs. Even if this describes you, a Real Estate Limited Partnership is probably too speculative to be an effective *Just Don't Lose the Money* type of investment.

Raw Land – Raw, undeveloped land has an awful lot going against it as a good option for the *Just Don't Lose the Money* investor. To start with, taxes are high and no depreciation is allowed. It is also highly speculative in nature. Unless you are an experienced real estate developer who has a proven success record in purchasing raw land and turning it into profits, stay far away from any "opportunity" to invest in raw land. The end result will likely be lost money.

Just Don't Lose the Money Tip
Avoid Probate

Avoiding probate for passing on any investment or vacation real estate you own is as important as avoiding probate for passing on your personal real estate. You can place these types of real estate into a trust the same way you can place personal real estate into a trust, with the same benefits (see Chapter 11 for details about trusts). You can also place these types of real estate into a Life Estate (see Chapter 5 for details about Life Estates), with the same benefits and limitations that affect personal real estate placed into a Life Estate.

A QUICK REVIEW

1 The value of vacation homes lies more in the personal enjoyment they provide than in any real short-term financial return. You can rent a vacation home for up to 14 days a year without reporting the income, and sell a qualified vacation home with the same tax breaks on the profits you get selling a primary residence. If you do buy a vacation home, treat it as a luxury rather than as an investment that will produce a return. Still look to maximize your financial gain by investing in a vacation home that will offer good potential rental and resale value. Vacation property can be used in a retirement "downsizing" strategy.

2 Rental property offers numerous tax write-offs against rental income. One tax downside is that all profits from the sale of rental property that is used solely for rental purposes (as opposed to property that is rented part of the time and used by you or your family the rest of the time) are taxable. While rental property can be an excellent long-term investment, keep in mind that as a landlord you must provide or pay for all repairs, maintenance, and upkeep. These costs will likely reduce your profits from rental income by a significant amount, although you can partially recoup them as tax write-offs. Remember, be a strong landlord.

3 Real Estate Investment Trusts (REITs) operate like mutual funds that pool investors' money to purchase real estate holdings. REITs can offer high dividends but are also usually expensive. They can represent a good investment but require careful research and expert advice before making a purchase. Real Estate Limited Partnerships and raw land purchases are complex, high-risk investments best avoided by all but seasoned real estate and development professionals.

The Best Four Years of Their Lives
Paying for Grandkids' (or Kids')
College Education

One of the greatest gifts you can give a child or grandchild is education. Whether it is college, trade school, or beauty school, it doesn't matter. To give a child the tools to be financially independent is a goal we all have. Sometimes college is not the answer. You can't fit a square peg into a round hole, but to help pay for further development such as a trade or night school almost always reaps dividends. Of course, many times you can lead a horse to water but you can't make it drink... but you can try. A gift that brings independence is the goal. A gift that acts like a crutch is of no use to anyone.

Depending on your age, you may remember a time when college was a nice luxury if you could afford it, but most people didn't go. You could start out in the mailroom, work hard, and years later, if you had the talent, wind up as a vice president with a corner office.

Those days are over. While it is still possible to make a decent living with a high school diploma if you are a skilled tradesperson, everyone else needs a college degree or some type of training if they hope to land a decent paying job. If you start out in the mailroom with a high school degree, there's a good chance that's where you'll be 20 years later. It may not be fair, but it's a fact of life in the 21st century.

Naturally the last thing you want to see your grandkids (or possibly kids, depending on what stage(s) in life you had children) do is spend their lives trapped in a low-wage, unfulfilling job. So you may want to help them pay for their college expenses. Depending on how recently you looked at the current cost of typical college expenses, you may be in for a bit of a shock.

Along with health care, the cost of higher education has been soaring well beyond the rate of inflation for the past 20 years or so. According to CollegeBoard.com, the average yearly cost for a four-year private college in the 2006-07 academic year was $22,218. The comparable yearly cost for a four-year public college was $5,836, though this varies significantly by region of the country (i.e., you'll pay a lot more for a four-year public college in the Northeast) and other factors.

Both price tags rose approximately six percent from the 2005-06 academic year, well above the rate of inflation. And there is no sign of these costs slowing down for 2007-08, or for any other time period in the near future.

Okay, take a deep breath. We're not suggesting that you take your intellectually gifted, mechanically declined kid, stick a wrench in his hand, and send him off to make his fortune in the trades. What we are suggesting is that if you want to help pay for a college education, start saving early. As soon as the child is born is preferable, but if it's too late for that, today would be a great time to start saving.

Fortunately, there are a number of effective ways to save for a college education that you can choose from. Some savings programs are provided by state or federal government, and some are provided by private industry. We are not going to get into financial aid, scholarships, or loans here—just tax-advantaged investment vehicles that will help you set aside money and let it grow to ease some of the financial burden that college can inflict. We will begin by examining the 529 Plan, a popular state-sponsored college savings program.

529 PLAN

Each state offers its own variety of college savings programs, but every state provides a version of the standardized state-sponsored college investment offering known as the 529 Plan. Named after Section 529 of the Internal Revenue Code, the 529 Plan comes in two varieties: prepaid tuition and savings.

The prepaid tuition 529 Plan allows you to pay the current rate of tuition at a state school, either as a lump sum or in installments, to cover a child's expenses in the future. The details of a how a 529 Plan is administered vary from state to state, but most allow out-of-state investors to participate. If a child does not go to college after tuition has already been prepaid, that money can be transferred to be used for a sibling with no fee. However, if the money winds up not being used for college tuition, there is usually a withdrawal penalty.

Money invested in a prepaid tuition 529 Plan does not "grow" in the strict sense. To determine your return, compare the percentage of tuition inflation between the time you prepay the tuition and the time the plan beneficiary (kid) enters college. Bear in mind that any money spent on prepaid tuition reduces your financial aid eligibility dollar for dollar.

There is another version of the prepaid tuition 529 Plan known as the Independent 529 Plan. It works similarly to a state plan, except that the money you invest can be used to pay future tuition at any participating private college. Your investment represents a percentage (up to 100 percent) of a school's current tuition.

For example, if you prepay $10,000 to cover one year of tuition and your child winds up attending a school that currently costs $20,000 a year, you will be covered for 50 percent of the tuition cost. If by the time your child attends annual tuition has risen to $40,000, you will only owe $20,000, essentially saving $10,000 in increased tuition for your initial $10,000 investment. You get your money back if your child doesn't attend a participating college, with annual return capped at 2 percent.

The savings 529 Plan allows you to invest money and have it grow tax-deferred until the beneficiary is ready to enter college. Think of it like a Roth IRA plan for college savings. Although your contributions are not tax-deductible, your investment grows tax-deferred, and distributions to pay for college costs are tax-free. In addition to the tax benefits, you stay in control of the account and make sure Junior does not blow the money on a new Porsche. These plans typically invest in mutual funds, and many offer age-based allocation strategies that invest your money more conservatively the closer the beneficiary gets to college age. You can also normally maintain a fixed equity-to-income ratio for the duration of the plan, if you choose, and some plans feature a principal protection option.

Some states exempt qualified withdrawals from savings 529 Plans from state income tax, and money can be used for tuition, fees, room, board, books, and other required equipment (many colleges now mandate that each student have a laptop computer). You are not required to invest in an in-state savings 529 Plan.

Overall, both varieties of 529 Plan provide many advantages to families saving for a child's college education. Some observers have questioned the fees charged by savings 529 Plans as compared to the fees charged by other investment vehicles, but as always, do your homework, shop around, and speak with a financial professional before participating.

COVERDELL EDUCATION SAVINGS ACCOUNT (ESA)

Named after the late Georgia Senator Paul Coverdell, the Coverdell ESA, formerly known as the Education IRA, is a tax-advantaged college savings account that in many ways operates like a savings 529 Plan. Unlike a savings 529 Plan, it is not state-sponsored, but money grows tax-deferred in the same way, and withdrawals for qualified college expenses are completely tax-free. The rules for investment are the same as those for an IRA, without the limits imposed by many 529 plans.

Another major differentiator between Coverdell ESAs and 529 Plans is that there is an annual contribution limit for Coverdell ESAs, currently $2,000 per year per child. This amount can be less depending on the income of the ESA contributor. And unlike a 529 Plan, money from a Coverdell ESA can also be used to pay for qualified elementary and secondary school expenses. Consult a qualified financial advisor to see if a Coverdell ESA would be the best way for to you to save for a child's college expenses.

ZERO-COUPON BONDS

As described in Chapter 3, zero-coupon bonds pay the holder no interest until maturity (as opposed to conventional bonds that pay interest every six months), but generally sell at a significant discount from face value. Their predictable payout and substantial advance discount make them an attractive option for many people saving for college. With proper timing, you can also purchase a zero-coupon bond that will mature at the same time a child is entering college.

As we also previously explained, even though interest on a zero-coupon bond is not paid until maturity, the holder is still liable for annual taxes on the "phantom" interest that accrues, unless you purchase a municipal zero-coupon bond. You can also place a zero-coupon bond in an IRA to avoid "phantom" interest payments.

Another way to minimize the tax burden of a zero-coupon bond being used to pay for college is to use the "kiddie tax" to your advantage. The kiddie tax is an IRS requirement for children under 14 to pay their parents' tax rate (as opposed to their own lower child's tax rate) on all unearned income (such as bond interest) exceeding a specified level that is regularly adjusted. There is an initial tax-free unearned income threshold, a second threshold where the child pays his or her own tax rate, and then the "kiddie tax" threshold where the parents' rate kicks in.

Because of the way compound interest works, a zero-coupon bond bought in a child's name at their birth will pay lower interest during their "kiddie tax" years, when they are susceptible to paying their parent's tax rate at a certain income threshold, and more interest in their later years, when all their unearned income is taxed at their own lower rate. Thus by investing in a zero-coupon bond early, you can minimize taxes on the interest.

U.S. SAVINGS BONDS

As mentioned in Chapter 3, a U.S. Savings Bond is the safest bond investment you can make. It carries a zero default risk, which is very nice when you are making an investment in something as crucial as a college education. Of course, this lack of risk also translates into low-interest payments. However, a U.S. Savings Bond allocated for college expenses carries some tax advantages that help offset the minimal growth it represents for your investment.

If a U.S. Savings Bond is bought in the name of a parent who is at least 24 years old when it is purchased and its interest is used to pay college tuition or fees (no books, dormitory costs, etc.), that interest can become entirely or partially tax-free. Tax savings, if any, depend on the parent's modified adjusted gross income, and at higher levels the tax advantage vanishes. Check with a financial advisor to see if your family would qualify for a tax break on U.S. Savings Bond interest used to pay for college expenses.

EDUCATIONAL TRUSTS

Imagine your child or grandchild at their college graduation, looking all spiffy in their cap and gown and beaming with pride as they accept their diploma. Hopefully this is something you will get to see in person. But what if you don't?

Especially if you had a child later in life or are saving for the education of a grandchild (or even great-grandchild), you may pass away before that child completes or even enters college. How can you ensure that assets you set aside for their education are used for that purpose and do not get depleted by probate fees and estate taxes? Set up an educational trust.

We will cover trusts in detail in Chapter 11. Simply put, a trust is a legal entity that allows you to hold and manage your assets both during and after your lifetime. Whatever assets you place into a trust (any type of asset you can think of, such as cash, stocks, bonds, mutual funds, real estate, etc.) become property of the trust. The trust is managed by a trustee, who can be a family member or a paid professional, depending on your preference. Either way, the trustee is legally obligated to act for the trust beneficiaries, who you also name.

To create an educational trust, simply name a child who will be going to college someday as the beneficiary. You can dictate how you would like the assets to be invested and spent. This means that the beneficiary will be able to withdraw money for approved college expenses, but not to pay for a spring break trip to Cancun.

Furthermore, if you do pass away before the child enters or graduates college, the assets inside it will not be subject to estate tax or probate if the trust was setup properly. To provide an extra incentive to study hard and get that piece of paper, you can make the remainder of the trust payable to the child as a lump sum or in installments after they have completed their degree.

Just Don't Lose the Money Tip
Start Early!

The gift of education is one of the greatest gifts you can give. It helps make kids independent contributing members of society and not a financial burden. Grown children who do not need financial help are another way of "just not losing the money."

We cannot stress enough the importance of saving for college early. While college costs may not continue growing at the break-neck pace of the past two decades forever, it is a safe bet that they will continue to rise at a noticeable rate for years to come. With the world becoming more complex and dependent on advanced technology, there is no reason to think the value of a college degree will fade anytime soon.

If you have a life insurance policy with a cash reserve or investment plan (see Chapter 9 for details), you can dedicate the returns in later years to paying for college expenses. If your life insurance plan has a surrender value, you may consider cashing it in toward the end of the plan and using that money for college expenses, as well. Before doing this, make sure you are covered for all risks. Consult a financial professional before canceling any life insurance.

A QUICK REVIEW

1 College costs have been growing well past the rate of inflation for many years and are now at the point where a year of college may cost upwards of $30,000. A college degree has also become mandatory to achieve success in today's knowledge-based economy. This means that you must begin saving for college as soon as possible, preferably when a child is born or even beforehand.

2 Each state offers a form of the 529 Plan, a college savings program that comes in two varieties. The prepaid tuition 529 Plan allows you to pay today's tuition rates for a child to attend a state college in the future, with the return determined by tuition inflation. The savings 529 Plan allows you to invest money and have it grow tax-deferred, with some plans allowing you to avoid state income tax for qualified withdrawals. Return is not guaranteed, though some plans offer principal protection. Coverdell Education Savings Accounts are similar to savings 529 Plans. There is also an Independent 529 Plan that allows you to prepay a percentage of tuition at participating private schools.

3 To ensure that money saved for college will be spent for college, even after your death, you can open an educational trust. This will also allow assets being saved for college to pass to your beneficiary in the event of your death, without estate tax or probate. You can set up rules in the trust to ensure that money is only used for approved educational expenses and that the beneficiary doesn't collect the remainder until they receive a diploma.

Think Twice
Risky Investments

Life is not a sprint. It is a marathon. Early on, one can afford to take some risk because you have time to recover. Remember playing baseball, kickball, skiing, running, etc. when you were a kid? You pushed yourself. You took risks by playing too hard or too long — you got sore and hurt. You were young and your body recovered. When you are older, try to do the same thing and your body might not ever recover. It's the same with money. There is a time to take risks and a time to stay away from risks because you have little recovery time. Remember you are not 20 years old forever.

When we named our book *Just Don't Lose the Money*, it wasn't an idle choice of title. We thought long and hard about how to succinctly express the philosophy we lay out in these pages. *Just Don't Lose the Money* really says it all.

More important than obtaining fast growth or even high long-term returns is developing an investment strategy that provides you with a safe shelter that will maintain what you have spent your life earning and protect it from taxes and other expenses as much as possible. In the past seven chapters, we have investigated a variety of investment options that, when properly employed, provide the best opportunity to avoid losing what you put into them.

Despite our best efforts, we understand that our readers are human and may still find themselves drawn by the lure of riskier, high-return investments. This is perfectly understandable. Determining risk is not an exact science.

Once you get past the investments that carry zero or virtually no risk, such as FDIC-insured bank accounts, U.S. government-issued bonds, and fixed tax-deferred annuities, it can become a little tricky to measure the risk of one investment against another. And there is no concrete formula to determine exactly when "acceptable" risk turns into "unacceptable" risk.

To help you navigate the murky waters of higher-risk investments, in this chapter we will review some of the more common vehicles that provide a greater upside along with a greater downside. We will explain why they are best left alone by the prudent investor who follows the *Just Don't Lose the Money* principles set forth in this book.

If you find the temptation of higher-risk investments irresistible, allocate a limited percentage of your portfolio to them and make sure you only use money you can afford to lose. The idea of spending your retirement in a villa on a private beach may be appealing, but is it really worth taking the chance when reaching for that villa may expose you to the possibility of spending your retirement in a cramped apartment in the inner city?

Here are a few risky investments you should use extreme caution before undertaking, assuming you don't take the safer route and ignore them completely.

FOREIGN REAL ESTATE, CURRENCY OR OTHER HOLDINGS

Billionaire George Soros is famous for having made much of his fortune by speculating in British currency. He essentially gambled against the Bank of England and won in a big way. To paraphrase a famous line from the 1988 vice-presidential debates, you're no George Soros.

Speculating in American currency is risky enough, but entering a foreign market multiplies the risk many times over. Even in the case of First World capitalist societies such as Great Britain, you are still navigating a complex set of rules and regulations that may be quite different than those in the U.S.

The same is even truer for investments in foreign real estate, securities, or other holdings. Keep in mind that despite the nearly universal complaint American citizens have about our taxes, compared to most of the world our tax rates are actually low. Investing in foreign property may expose you to extremely high taxes that could wipe out most or all of whatever advantage you thought you were gaining.

Furthermore, if any legal issues crop up, you will be remotely dealing with an unfamiliar legal system that is not likely to be tilted in the favor of non-resident, non-citizens. Once again, even if you are investing in a First World democracy, you may still come across laws regarding finances, property ownership, liability, taxes, and other issues that are markedly different than the U.S., where laws tend to favor investment and development. If you want to do some international investing, find a reputable mutual fund that includes international holdings. The fund will employ experts to navigate the tricky global investment waters and also substantially dilute any risk your money may be exposed to.

Just Don't Lose the Money Tip
Stay Away From These Types of Investments

Speculative investments

Many opportunities exist for you to sink your money into speculative investments. These are business ventures with no certain outcome, such as prospecting for oil in unproven fields or opening a new mine in a spot where there is presumed to be valuable metals or ores. There are a variety of investment funds that specialize in these types of ventures, or you may even have the opportunity to directly invest in a company that has mineral rights in a certain untapped area.

Granted, the upside to these types of ventures can be almost limitless. There are worse things in the world than being the part owner of a successful oil field. One slight problem exists with speculative investments, however: They almost always fail.

Simply put, the odds of a neophyte striking it rich in this type of speculation are virtually nil. You simply don't have the proper background or training to perform the proper due diligence on a speculative investment, to sort out the rare good opportunity from the all-too-common wild goose chase or even downright fraud. Beware of ads that talk about "secrets of profiting" or "make a fortune" from oil wells or similar ventures.

Think back to our advice in Chapter 6 about investing in raw land. Unless you're an expert real estate developer, don't do it. The same applies here. Did you spend 25 years as an executive in a mining concern? You may be able to make an intelligent decision regarding a speculative mining venture. Otherwise, forget it.

Art

There is an old saying that goes, "I may not know art, but I know-what I like." That is a useful approach to take toward art investments. What we mean by that is, buy art for purely decorative purposes. As one collector put it, "You don't own art, rather, art owns you." If you like it and can afford it as a luxury expense, by all means buy it. If you think a particular piece of artwork will skyrocket in value in the coming years and provide you with an easy retirement, don't bother. It's always easier to buy than to sell.

Art is extremely fickle. Today's hot painter could become the tired old cliché of tomorrow, and a stone carving that is considered junk now could become the most brilliant example of early 21st century sculpture in 30 years. The value of art is based upon, among other things, popular opinion; the opinion of art scholars, critics and other experts; marketing by art dealers and agents; and to some extent, whether the artist in question is alive or dead. Do you really feel comfortable risking the comfort and happiness of your post-retirement years on these unpredictable factors?

Art is another investment opportunity best left to the experts. Maybe you owned an art gallery and really know what to look for in investment-quality art. In that case, art speculation may pay off for you. If you do have a decent collection, consider consulting an art advisor who works with collectors of art and antiques, their financial advisors and the charitable organizations they support to plan for the disposition of these assets. A recent book by Michael Mendelsohn called *Life Is Short, Art Is Long* is a great resource for people researching the financial aspects of art. Even if you are a legitimate expert in the field, keep in mind that there are limited tax advantages related to art investments and you must pay the ongoing costs of insuring and storing your artwork. When you do sell, any profits you make are fully taxable at the 28 percent capital gains rate...Doesn't an IRA start to look a little more appealing?

Precious metals

For centuries, mankind has been fascinated by gold and silver. One of the main reasons the Spanish conquistadors came to the New World was to seek "El Dorado," the legendary city of gold, and the value of U.S. currency was once backed by gold. Popular wisdom dictates that in times of war or crisis (such as today), the value of precious metals goes up, as gold and silver represent a "sure thing."

As a popular 1980s rap group once said, "don't believe the hype." Historically, gold's performance against inflation has been poor, even taking spikes related to world events into account. Whenever gold values rise too rapidly, central banks, which hold about 20 percent of the world's gold supply, can quickly sell off their gold holdings, depressing the price almost immediately. Periods of inflation can lead to spikes in the price of gold, but inevitably this leads to a bubble in the commodities market that pops like in the early 1980s. Some people may make money with short-term gold investment strategies, but you can probably guess by now what we think of this type of speculative investment.

Silver is an even poorer investment choice than gold. The silver market is a small one and supply generally outstrips demand. The market is small enough to be vulnerable to "cornering," a situation whereby a single investor or small group of investors buys up enough of a marketplace to dominate it and manipulate its price. This happened in the late 1970s and early 1980s, resulting in negative consequences for silver investors and the world economy in general. Gold and silver make very nice jewelry, but lousy financial investments.

Antiques/Collectibles
All the rules that apply to art apply to antiques and other collectibles, perhaps even more so. The collectibles market is highly susceptible to short-lived fads and crazes. Remember when it was hard to find a Beanie Baby in a store? Or how about the baseball memorabilia craze of the early 1990s?

Public interest in antiques and collectibles has been piqued by television shows where experts tell people random junk they found in their attic is worth thousands of dollars, and by tales of people who make small fortunes buying items cheaply at yard sales and selling them online for huge markups. Many of these stories are true, but they represent the exception, not the rule.

Antiques and collectibles also represent an investment category with limited tax breaks and associated insurance and storage expenses. In short, buy that 19th century end table because it will look nice in your living room, not because you think its resale value will finance your new boat someday.

Futures/ Commodities

Futures exchanges are speculative investment markets where you promise to buy shares of a commodity tomorrow at a price you set today. You are betting against the seller that the future price of the commodity, such as oil or pork bellies, will be higher than what you are agreeing to pay. The seller is most likely an expert in that particular commodity. You are most likely not. Guess who usually wins in this gamble?

Investing in futures is one of the riskiest investments you can make, period. Even for an expert, there is no way to accurately predict how future weather, pestilence, warfare, or other calamities may affect the price of a given commodity. They are playing the game with one eye open, you're playing blind. Leave futures to the pros. Trying to gauge the fair price of an investment today is tough enough without attempting to be psychic about it.

Stock options and other unconventional maneuvers

Buying a stock option gives you the right, but not the obligation, to buy or sell a stock by a certain future date at a fixed price. You do not have to actually exercise the option, and it typically expires within six months. A call option gives the holder the right to purchase a stock at a specific price within a certain period of time. A put option, by contrast, gives the holder the right to sell a stock at a specific price within a certain period of time. The options investor pays a fee called an option premium to obtain this right.

A put option is often known as "selling short." This is an investment strategy where you try to make money from a market decline, since you're hoping that the price of the stock drops below the price agreed upon in your put option. Then you can sell the stock at the higher price in the put option and profit from the difference. Otherwise you will lose money on the put, since even if you don't sell it you still must pay the option premium.

Another short-selling strategy is to borrow a stock at a certain price, sell it immediately, buy it back when the price drops, and then return the shares to the original owner while pocketing the difference. You must complete these transactions within a specified timeframe, which is inherently risky.

Calls, on the other hand, are useful if you believe a given stock is likely to increase in value. If the price of the stock rises beyond the purchase price quoted in the call, you could purchase the stock at the lower price and then sell it at a profit. If the price of the stock declines, you can opt not to purchase it but you will still be out the cost of the option.

Sound complicated? It is. Making money on put or call options is not easy. Like commodities futures, these types of speculative stock investments are best left to expert brokers. A straightforward purchase of a reputable mutual fund or blue chip stock is a much better way to protect your stock market investments.

A QUICK REVIEW

1 *Just Don't Lose the Money* is a mindset that precludes most risky investments. While speculation, precious metals, and other higher-risk investments may present the chance to make a large short-term profit, they do not lend themselves to long-term financial planning and offer little recourse if a loss occurs.

2 Investments in foreign currency, real estate, or other international holdings require an in-depth knowledge of how the laws and customs of a foreign country work. Even if you possess this knowledge, legal issues may be extremely complex and if you have legal problems, you may have little or no standing in a foreign court. Also keep in mind that most foreign countries have complicated tax codes that may eat up most or all of your profits.

3 Any type of investment that involves predicting the short-term future value of a commodity or stock is exceedingly risky. Even financial experts have no way to predict how uncontrollable events such as weather and strife may affect the value of a commodity or stock. So unless you are a seasoned investor, it is best to avoid the futures and options markets.

Just Don't Lose the Money Tip
Don't Do It All, or Tread Lightly

The safest way to deal with any of the investments we have covered in this chapter is to avoid them completely. However, if you absolutely must dabble in a higher-risk investment, keep your involvement to dabbling level. Allocate no more than five percent of your investment portfolio to these types of holdings.

Also make sure that any money you invest in them is money that you can absolutely live without. Treat these investments the way you would a bet at a casino: you are basically facing the same odds.

Covering Your Bases

Insurance

When you have nothing to lose, you have no risk. When you have something to lose, you have risk. How do you cover your losses, such as your house burning down and premature death? You buy money. Insurance is buying money. You give the insurance company $1 and if your house burns down, they give you $25. It is that simple. Insurance is a necessary part of our financial well-being.

Insurance can be a funny investment. In many cases, it may be an investment you make hoping it doesn't pay off. For example, how many people really want to experience catastrophic damage to their residence to get the most out of the money they sunk into homeowners' insurance? But it's far better to have insurance and not need it than to need insurance and not have it.

Going through life under- or uninsured is a surefire way to lose the money. The costs of things like home repair, prescription drugs, and medical care can quickly overwhelm even the most prudent investor if they carry no insurance to defray the bill. And in another completely unscientific observation that somehow always proves itself true, the people without insurance seem to wind up needing it the most.

In this chapter, we will review several types of insurance that everyone should carry. Some, like Medicare, are only available to seniors, while others are available without age restriction. But you need to be familiar with all the different types of insurance you need, and have completed all the necessary research and preparation long before you make any investments.

PROTECT YOUR MOST IMPORTANT ASSET: LIFE INSURANCE

Ask most people what their most important asset is, and you will probably get an answer like "my home" or "my 401(k)." But when you really think about it, what's more valuable than your life? Not just to you, but to your loved ones? Besides the terrible emotional loss that your death would create for your family, think about the financial loss that would result.

You can no longer create any type of income (unless you have royalties or image rights you can pass along!), and without proper planning your beneficiaries may have to wade through a maze of taxes and probate proceedings before they can inherit anything you have left behind for them. Life insurance can provide a solution to all these problems, and even provide a return on investment while you're alive. The lump sum a life insurance policy pays upon your death is subject to estate tax if your estate is greater than your credits (see Chapter 11), but some advance planning can minimize the impact.

Before deciding which variety of life insurance policies best fits your needs, you need to first determine how much income you will be replacing. Determine how much money your family will need both in the short-term, to cover immediate bills as well as funeral expenses and other costs associated with your death, and long-term to maintain the standard of living they're used to.

When determining how much money your family will need after you're gone, also keep in mind that after they pay off whatever bills need immediate attention, they should invest the remainder of the money to produce a steady income stream. Try to develop a rough calculation of the annual return they would get from a safe, "just don't lose the money" type of investment plan with the settlement. Also keep possible future costs like college education in mind.

After figuring out what income you will need to replace and what major expenses your family will likely be facing in the years after you're gone, it is time to select a basic type of life insurance policy. Some policies are very simple and pay a fixed lump sum, others are more complex and may offer a variable return or investment feature. Consult with a qualified insurance expert before purchasing any form of life insurance. A brief summary of the major types of available life insurance policies follows.

Term Life – The simplest form of life insurance, a term life policy insures your life for a certain amount of money for a fixed period of time (typically one year). You pay an annual premium based on your age, health, and coverage amount. Typically your premiums will rise as you grow older. There are level premium policies where the yearly premium will stay the same for 5, 10, 20, or even 30 years.

There are no savings or investment features to a term life insurance policy—if you outlive the policy, you don't get any money back, you can't convert the policy to cash, and beneficiaries can only collect the money if you die before the term expires. Some term life policies may offer a return-of-premium feature allowing you to collect the premiums you paid if you outlive the term of the contract.

Annual Renewable Term Life – This operates the same as a term life insurance policy, except that you purchase it as a series of one-year policies. The insurance company guarantees you the right to purchase new one-year policies without an additional physical exam. Rates will rise each year.

Guaranteed Level Term Life – With this form of a term life insurance policy, your premiums start higher but remain level for a certain number of years, allowing you to save money in later years of the contract.

Declining Term Life – Also known as a decreasing or reducing term life insurance policy, declining term life insurance allows your coverage and premiums to grow smaller during the length of the contract.

Convertible Term Life – This requires higher premiums than a regular term life insurance policy but allows you to convert your policy to a whole life insurance policy (see details below) without an additional physical exam.

Whole Life – Also known as ordinary life insurance, it has both an insurance component and an investment component. Whole life insurance provides a set amount of permanent insurance with a premium that remains fixed throughout the policy term. In the early years of the contact, the premium you pay exceeds the actual costs of the policy.

The extra premium and interest goes into a cash reserve fund (the investment component), of which part pays maintenance costs and part gets credited to your account and earns dividends.

After a few years, the interest builds tax-free, creating a cash value you can borrow against, purchase another policy with, pay premiums with, or claim by surrendering your rights to the policy. Any loans you take out against the policy will be paid off from the settlement or surrender amount before it is distributed.

Variable Life – Variable life insurance is similar to whole life insurance, except that it allows you to invest your accumulated cash value in mutual fund-type investments instead of fixed-return investments. If your investments perform poorly, you can lose the death benefit down to a guaranteed minimum amount, and you can also lose part of the cash value. You decide how much of the net premium to invest. Variable life insurance is technically considered a security, and is a higher-risk, higher-return form of investment.

Universal Life – Similar to variable life insurance, universal life insurance offers bonds or other low-risk investment options, rather than mutual fund-type investment options for the investment component of the policy. You can select a variable premium and face amount for the policy, and build cash value with guaranteed minimum interest. However, the lower premiums associated with a universal life insurance policy means the cash value will be lower than what you normally receive with a whole or variable life insurance policy.

Universal Variable Life – Essentially, this is variable life insurance with a wider range of investment options. You have the flexibility to raise and lower premiums, and direct as much of your premium as you want to an investment account that grows tax-free until you withdraw it.

Bear in mind that there is no guarantee to any of your investment in a universal variable life insurance policy, meaning that you can lose all your premiums as well as all your interest! For this reason we would generally caution the *Just Don't Lose the Money* investor against relying on universal variable life insurance. However, some universal life policies (for example, the Keepsake 201 plan from Aviva Life Insurance) offer guarantees beyond the typical universal life policy. You make a one-time premium payment (meaning you make a single lump sum payment upfront) and you are guaranteed a return of the full cash value if you need it. As always, consult with a financial professional if you are considering this type of investment.

Second-to-Die Insurance – A second-to-die policy (also known as a survivorship policy) does not pay out when you die. Rather, it insures two lives, usually a husband and wife. The death benefit is not paid until both of the insured pass on. These policies often have lower premiums than you would find for a singled insured. The second-to-die policy is also useful to help pay estate taxes on the couple's other assets upon the death of both spouses. The second-to-die policy is often combined with an Irrevocable Life Insurance Trust (ILIT) to avoid estate taxes on the proceeds from the policy (see Chapter 11 for details). Ownership of the policy is transferred to the ILIT. Once named, beneficiaries to an ILIT are irrevocable, which means their status can only be changed with their permission. ILIT beneficiaries pay no income or estate taxes on the proceeds, and it does not pass through probate. The cash from the ILIT can be paid as a lump sum, as interest only (principal remains with the insurance company and can be withdrawn at will), as fixed installments with interest, or as life income based on the beneficiaries' age and amount of the proceeds.

As you can see, there are numerous options for your life insurance coverage, each with its own advantages and disadvantages. If you are most concerned with simply replacing your income in the event of your demise, some form of term life insurance is probably your best option.

If you are looking to create a long-term investment that can offer financial benefit during your lifetime as well as after it, then you probably want to consider whole, variable, or universal life insurance. Whole life insurance in particular offers safeguards against excessive risk to your investment while still offering reasonable returns. If estate taxes are a concern, consider transferring ownership of the policy into an ILIT.

CREATING WEALTH

One interesting method of using life insurance is creating wealth for the next generation. Life insurance is like buying dollars with quarters. You give an insurance company 25 cents and then when you die, they give your heirs $1.00.

An example would be a 70-year-old couple that pays a $10,000 premium for 10 years ($100,000 total) and ends up with a guaranteed life insurance policy of $1 million that, with proper planning, goes to their heirs on a tax-free basis.

So there are some very creative ways you can use an old-fashioned product and create wealth that can benefit generations to come.

WEALTH REPLACEMENT TRUSTS – LIFE INSURANCE AND YOUR FAVORITE CHARITY

Life insurance is particularly valuable when you are younger and still working, as you are actively producing an income that your family at least partially depends upon for their well-being. After you retire, however, the need to replace annual income wanes or disappears, and most of your other income-producing vehicles are investments that can be directly passed along to your beneficiaries. Also, if you have purchased a life insurance policy that carries a surrender value, this may be the time to consider collecting it.

At the later stages of your life, it may make sense to switch from life insurance to a wealth replacement trust. A wealth replacement trust is a form of a charitable remainder trust, which is an irrevocable trust (see Chapter 11 for details) that has a charity of your choice designated as the beneficiary. The property within the trust is sold and reinvested to create a lifetime income for you. You receive tax advantages on your investment because it is ultimately going to a charity.

In a regular charitable remainder trust, the charity becomes the trust beneficiary at the time of your death and your loved ones do not receive any of the proceeds. In a wealth replacement trust, you use a portion of your lifetime income to buy a life insurance policy to replace the value of the assets within the trust and name your loved ones as beneficiaries. The life insurance can be held in its own separate irrevocable trust.

Because the trust owns the policy, its value will pass to the named beneficiaries without being subject to estate tax. In essence, you are using life insurance not to replace lost income, but to provide a tax-free substitute for otherwise taxable assets your beneficiaries would inherit, and you pick up further tax advantages on your investment to boot. As with any major investment decision, consult a financial professional before opening a wealth replacement trust.

WEALTH REPLACEMENT TRUST: LIFE INSURANCE AND YOUR FAMILY – AN ALTERNATIVE TO LONG-TERM CARE INSURANCE

To many people, charity begins at home—your children and grand-children. Life insurance can sometimes be used as an alternative to long-term care insurance.

As explained in this chapter, traditional long-term care insurance is essentially buying a bucket of money to pay for long-term care medical costs so that you can protect your estate. One problem people perceive with long-term care insurance is that if you don't use the insurance you've paid all those premiums for nothing. An alternative to long-term care insurance is to use a life insurance policy inside a wealth replacement trust.

As an example, let's say that you estimate the cost of long-term care at $500,000 ($100,000 per year for five years). For this example, let's assume you have $500,000 in the bank. The strategy is to take out a life insurance policy for $500,000 and put that policy in a wealth replacement trust. If you go into a nursing home and spend your own $500,000, then when you pass away your heirs get the $500,000 life insurance proceeds that "replaces" the money you used for your long-term care. If you never go into a nursing home, your family gets the $500,000 in the bank AND the $500,000 in the trust.

Life insurance has come a long way over the years. You can now get "custom made" guaranteed policies. You can choose a premium plan that allows you to pay a premium for a specific period of time ranging from one year to life. If, for instance, you chose a "10-year pay" guaranteed policy, the policy becomes self sufficient after 10 years, and no further premiums are needed.

USING LIFE INSURANCE INSTEAD OF A ROTH IRA

Another creative way of using life insurance is to use it as an alternative to a Roth IRA.

For example, if you're older and realize that you will not use all of your IRA money during retirement you might consider a Roth IRA.

If you qualify, you can take out more than your minimum required distribution, pay tax and put the proceeds in a Roth IRA. This would allow that amount to grow tax-free and be delivered to heirs tax-free.

The one problem with the above example is that the Roth IRA is still in your estate and can be subject to estate tax. In addition, it is still considered yours if you wind up in a nursing home.

If you are insurable, an alternative would be to take money out of your IRA in excess of your minimum distribution and put the proceeds in a life insurance policy. Life insurance also grows tax-free and is delivered to heirs tax-free, like a Roth.

If the life insurance is owned by an Asset Protection Trust, it is not subject to estate tax and protection from attachment of a nursing home is needed (after the look back period).

The creative use of life insurance is becoming more and more popular because of its unique tax treatment – which is NO tax.

Here's to Your Health: Private Health, Disability, and Long-term Care Insurance

If you are still working, hopefully your employer provides health insurance coverage and pays for a reasonable percentage of the cost. If you are self-employed, there are a variety of health insurance pools, usually set up to cover people in a similar profession, which can reduce the high cost of buying health insurance as an individual.

Simply put, you must carry health insurance to cover the day-to-day medical expenses of you and your family, as well as to cover the cost of injuries, illnesses, and other unforeseen incidents. Do not skimp! There are many flaws with our country's current managed healthcare system, but not carrying health insurance is about as certain a means to lose everything you have as you will find.

In addition to health insurance, you may want to carry extra disability insurance. This replaces income lost when you can't work due to illness or injury, and is not the same as worker's compensation insurance, which only covers injuries that happen within the scope of your employment. Some disability insurance policies will also cover part or all of approved rehabilitation costs resulting from an injury.

The amount of benefit disability insurance pays will vary depending on how much coverage you purchase and how high your premiums are. There is no single answer as to whether you should carry

Just Don't Lose the Money Tip

Universal Life Insurance vs. Long Term Care Insurance

As noted above, long-term care insurance is not the best investment if you do not end up needing long-term care. However, a new breed of life insurance has been developed which combines long-term care insurance inside a universal life insurance policy. The policy requires a single, one-time up-front payment on the premium and offers three key benefits. The first is a long-term care benefit that will provide funds for a nursing home, at-home care, assisted living care, or adult day care. The second benefit is life insurance. If you do not use the aforementioned long-term care benefit, there is a life insurance benefit paid tax-free to your heirs when you pass away. The third benefit is that if you cancel the policy at any time, you get all of your initial deposit back.

Unlike traditional long-term care policies, this type of universal life policy gives you life insurance, an investment component with tax-deferred growth, and provision for your long-term care, if necessary.

If you change your mind, you get your money back.

disability insurance, but if you engage in a high-risk profession (such as construction) or have a family history or lifestyle that predisposes you to certain risks, you should definitely consider it.

Keep in mind that premiums may be higher depending on your occupation or other variables, and that pre-existing conditions may make you ineligible for disability coverage. Also keep in mind that retirees are not eligible for disability insurance, although Social Security does offer disability payments to qualified recipients.

Private long-term care insurance covers the cost of long-term medical care in the event you need to enter a nursing home, assisted living facility, hospice, rehabilitation center, or other long-term care facility (see Chapter 10 for more details on how to properly protect yourself in case this ever becomes a necessity for you or your spouse). It may also cover the cost of qualified home healthcare services.

For retirees, private long-term care insurance acts as a supplement to Medicare (see below), which only covers nursing home care for 100 days and requires you to spend down your assets to qualify for long-term care coverage. Usually, long-term care insurance is offered as a fixed indemnity policy that offers lower premiums at younger ages.

Specific benefits vary with different long-term care insurance policies. Some policies offer built-in inflation protection to cover the rising rates of long-term health care. More recently, some policies have begun offering a return-of-premium feature that refunds part or all of the money you put in if you wind up not needing long-term care.

THE GOVERNMENT PITCHES IN: MEDICARE AND MEDIGAP

Medicare is a form of health insurance administered by the federal government for qualified individuals. To receive Medicare benefits, you must be 65 or older and eligible for either Social Security or railroad benefits. If you are under 65, you must have been on Social Security disability benefits for 24 months or suffer from chronic kidney disease.

While you cannot rely on Medicare alone to cover all your healthcare needs, it is a useful program that anyone eligible should take part in to help protect their assets against the often staggering cost of health care for older people.

There are four parts to Medicare: Parts A, B, C, and D. We will briefly review each part.

Part A: Hospital Insurance

Part A of Medicare is free for participants who have paid FICA-taxes for 40 or more quarters during their working career, so if you fit this description there is no excuse for not participating. You can also obtain Medicare Part A coverage for a premium if you do not meet eligibility requirements for free coverage.

Medicare Part A primarily pays for hospital stays and qualified stays in skilled nursing facilities. As mentioned above, Medicare will only cover 100 days of care in a skilled nursing facility (such as a nursing home), and requires a copayment after the first 20 days of free coverage. Part A will also pay for qualified post-hospital home health care costs.

Part B: Medical Insurance

Part B of Medicare pays for a set percentage of approved charges for doctors, home health aides, hospital outpatient treatment, lab tests, X-rays, physical therapy, and medical equipment. The Part B premium is deducted from your monthly Social Security check and there is also a yearly deductible.

You can enroll in Medicare Part B for up to three months before your 65th birthday, and doing so ensures that you start receiving coverage the first day of the month you turn 65. Each year that you wait past age 65 to enroll in Part B, the premium jumps by 10 percent, unless the delay is because you work past age 65 and are covered by a company health plan, or if you're covered by a spouse's health plan. Needless to say, waiting to enroll for any reason other than one that is approved flies in the face of the *Just Don't Lose the Money* mindset!

Part C: Medicare Advantage

To qualify for Medicare Part C, you must participate in Medicare Parts A and B. Medicare Part C is an alternative to Parts A and B that essentially allows you to receive Medicare services through a private insurer such as a Health Maintenance Organization (HMO). Medicare Part C usually offers additional coverage to what is provided in Parts A and B, with lower copayments.

Part D: Prescription Drug

Medicare Part D is the newest Medicare service, having gone into effect January 1, 2006 after a well-publicized Congressional debate and wrangling. Anyone who participates in Medicare Parts A and/ or B is eligible to participate in Part D. For a monthly premium deducted from your Social Security check, plus a yearly deductible, you receive a copayment for prescription drug costs.

To take advantage of Medicare Part D, you must participate in either a Prescription Drug Plan (PDP) or a Medicare Part C plan that includes prescription drug coverage. Plans are approved and regulated by the federal government, but delivered by private insurers, and not all plans offer the same benefits. Medicare specifically excludes certain drugs from Part D coverage.

Medigap

On average, Medicare covers about half of the typical recipient's medical bills. This leaves a lot of financial responsibility remaining on your shoulders. The federal government regulates a private insurance option known as "Medigap" that can help cover many of the healthcare costs and copayments that are left over by Medicare coverage.

Six months after you have enrolled in Medicare Part B, you are automatically eligible to receive Medigap insurance from any company that offers it. Policies vary by company as well as by state regulation, so you need to carefully research all available options before purchasing a Medigap plan. Some Medigap plans offer a copayment for nursing home care, but like Medicare, Medigap insurance will not indefinitely cover nursing home costs.

Like any government program, Medicare is subject to a fair amount of controversy and there are many questions over how effective it truly is and whether it will be financially viable in the long-term given the increase in number of retirees as the Baby Boomers start to retire. However, in the short-term it is the best and only option for many retirees, since fewer and fewer companies are providing any type of medical insurance or reimbursement options in their employee retirement packages.

Certainly if you qualify for free Medicare Part A coverage you would be foolish not to take advantage of it; and Medicare Part B coverage supplemented by some combination of Part D and/or Medigap, as well as private long-term care coverage, is strongly advisable for most retirees. It is easy to complain about Medicare, but harder for many retirees to find a workable alternative.

As we said before, not carrying health insurance, especially as you get older, is about as surefire a way to lose your money as you will find. If you are getting ready to retire, you need to thoroughly educate yourself about Medicare, particularly if you may want to enroll in Plan B, whose costs escalate the longer you wait after retiring to join.

BE IT EVER SO HUMBLE: HOMEOWNERS INSURANCE

No matter how humble your home may be: If you own it, you want to insure it. Homeowners insurance protects against losses due to events such as theft or fire, and also protects you against legal damages resulting from injuries or accidents occurring on the premises of your home.

A typical homeowners insurance policy covers your house and its contents, and may also reimburse you for additional living expenses or loss of rental income due to damages. Contents are usually figured as percentage of home value. Comprehensive personal liability covers damage to the property and lives of others caused by you anywhere you go or by an accident in your home.

Just Don't Lose the Money Tip
Don't Wait Too Long for Life Insurance (or Hold it Too Long)

Like so many other things in life, the essence of life insurance is timing. Do it while you are young to protect your income. Do it when you are older to protect your estate. The premiums you'll pay will vary with age and health. When you are older, there is good news and bad news about premiums. The bad news is that the premiums are bigger. The good news is that you can afford to pay them and you will be paying the premiums for less time.

When young, you should purchase life insurance as soon as someone besides you becomes dependent on your income. This means once you undergo a major life event such as getting married or having a child, it's time to get life insurance. You also probably want to buy life insurance if you are the primary source of income for a disabled or retired relative. In addition, some people may name a charity or educational institution the beneficiary of a life insurance policy.

On the flip side of this piece of advice, don't hold onto a life insurance policy too long. If you hold a policy with a surrender value and you reach the point you're reasonably sure you will outlive it, it's probably a good idea to cash it in or switch to another policy. That money can be reinvested in another *Just Don't Lose the Money*-approved investment vehicle.

Later in life, you may also want to investigate forming a wealth replacement trust, which essentially utilizes the proceeds from a life insurance policy inside a specially designed trust to replace any wealth you might have lost during your lifetime. The lost wealth can come from catastrophic health issues, estate taxes, or other unforeseen events.

New, enhanced guaranteed life insurance has become an important part of asset protection planning. Companies have developed unique products that allow for tax-free growth and tax-free distribution to heirs. You can even design your own policy. For example, you could set up an insurance policy that is guaranteed to age 110 even if you only want to pay into it for 10 years. Life insurance is essentially about buying tax-free dollars with quarters. The proper use of life insurance is a key *Just Don't Lose the Money* strategy.

Keep in mind that homeowners insurance coverage is generally limited to the policy owner and family members living in the covered house. In addition, compensation will only be for listed perils, meaning you cannot assume that damage from perils such as toxic mold will be automatically covered.

Moreover, floods and earthquakes are never covered by a standard policy and will always require separate coverage. If you own individual objects of great value, such as jewelry or other heirlooms, you can list them in separate riders on your policy to ensure proper coverage. To protect yourself against unexpected liens or claims to your property, you can purchase separate title insurance.

You have the choice of setting up your homeowners insurance policy to reimburse you for either the cash (depreciated) value of damaged property and assets, or the replacement (full new) value. You will pay higher premiums for a policy that reimburses you for replacement value.

Homeowners insurance is an absolute must. It is far too expensive to purchase and maintain a home, and legal judgments for even minor injuries are far too pricey, to consider risking going without homeowners insurance for even a moment. You should also supplement your homeowners insurance policy with an umbrella policy, which will provide extra coverage above the limits of your other policies, usually capped at $1 million, for low premiums. Furthermore, if you live in an area prone to earthquakes or floods, at least investigate your options for extra insurance to cover damages resulting from these calamities.

A QUICK REVIEW

1 There are three types of insurance you absolutely must carry: life, health, and homeowners. If you die without life insurance, (at least during your income-producing years) you will leave your beneficiaries with a huge financial loss; healthcare costs are too high for anyone to afford without help from insurance; and a home is far too expensive to leave unprotected in the event of damage or loss. Leaving yourself under- or uninsured is a sure path to losing your hard-earned savings.

2 There are many different life insurance options to meet different needs. The most basic life insurance option, term life, simply pays a lump sum based upon an annual premium, while other options (such as whole and variable) allow you to build a cash reserve that can be used for loans, investments, or to pay off premiums. No one type of life insurance is right for everyone, but you need to thoroughly determine your personal needs and your family's needs before purchasing any life insurance policy.

3 With average life expectancy on the rise and the need for long-term care consequently greater, people should consider insuring themselves with a combination life and long-term care policy. The benefit of this combination is threefold in that you not only receive life insurance, you also create the opportunity for tax-deferred investment growth along with long-term care coverage should it become necessary.

4 Medicare is a federal health insurance program available to retirees and other qualified Social Security recipients. Medicare Part A, which covers hospital bills, is free to qualified individuals. Medicare will typically only cover half your medical expenses and only offers limited coverage for nursing home care, but can be supplemented with various other insurance options and is generally a useful tool for retirees to help control their healthcare expenses.

5 Creative uses of life insurance include wealth replacement trusts and Roth IRA alternatives.

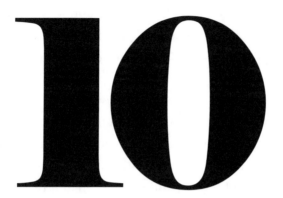

Worst-Case Scenario Planning
Nursing Home, Hospice, or Other Long-Term Care

Life should be simple. You are born, grow up, get a job, get married, have children, save money, retire, live well and then someday you die. Well, it isn't that simple. Some don't get married, some don't have children, some don't save money, some can't hold down a job, and some just don't grow up. The wild card in life is health. Health is wealth. Health, family and friends are even greater than material wealth. Asset protection strategies for long-term care and health issues are complex and must be age appropriate. What you do at age 60 is not the same as age 80. The goal is not to change your everyday life AND protect assets at the same time.

If you asked 100 people over age 65 what scares them the most, being "placed in a nursing home" would probably rank right up there with public speaking as a prospect that inspires absolute dread. This common fear often gets expressed as humor, as evidenced by the countless jokes and wisecracks that center on children getting their revenge through the nursing homes they choose for their parents.

Of course, nursing home care is no laughing matter. Families agonize over the emotionally devastating decision to place a parent, grandparent, or other loved one in a nursing home when their healthcare needs become overwhelming. Despite all the fears and jokes about substandard care and living conditions, there are many top-quality nursing homes, and nursing home care is often the most humane and responsible option for everyone involved.

The one truly scary aspect of nursing home care is the cost, which can often exceed $100,000 a year. Nursing home costs have skyrocketed even beyond the rapidly growing costs of higher education (see Chapter 7), and you cannot bank on being done with them after four years. These costs can quickly exhaust almost any savings portfolio, and without proper planning, the "spend down" requirements of Medicaid coverage can leave beneficiaries with little or nothing to inherit.

Fortunately, there are steps you can take to ensure that if you do someday require nursing home care, you can obtain it without losing your life savings. The key is to start making preparations now, long before you even think you may need nursing home care. The sooner you take steps to protect yourself against this "worst-case scenario," the better your odds of surviving it financially intact. Time is your most important asset with protection strategies.

MEDICAID – A BRIEF PRIMER

The federal and state governments jointly administer an insurance program called Medicaid (known as MassHealth in Massachusetts) that provides medical assistance to seniors, children, and disabled people who meet financial need requirements. This assistance can include nursing home and other forms of long-term care. As discussed in the previous chapter, Medicare will only cover up to 100 days of long-term care costs.

To qualify for Medicaid, you must meet eligibility requirements pertaining to your assets, income, estate, and property. These requirements are subject to changes in government regulations, so of course you should consult with a qualified financial professional before attempting to enroll in Medicaid.

Income Guidelines

The general rule under Medicaid is that you must pay all of your income to the nursing home with a couple of exceptions. For example, you can keep up to $72 per month for personal needs. If married, the healthy spouse can keep all of his or her own income as well as a portion of the nursing home bound spouse's income up to a certain amount, called the Minimum Monthly Maintenance Needs Allowance. This can cause a problem when one spouse with a pension goes into a nursing home. His or her pension goes with them thus depriving the stay-at-home spouse of needed income.

COUNTABLE AND NON-COUNTABLE ASSETS

A Medicaid recipient cannot have more than $2,000 in "countable" assets, although in some states (including Massachusetts) their "healthy" spouse may be able to have as much as $104,400 in countable assets, depending on state regulations.

The easiest way to determine if an asset is countable is to familiarize yourself with the categories of assets that are considered non-countable. These include personal property, autos, principal residences (for married couples), prepaid funerals, and "inaccessible" assets that are placed in irrevocable trusts. All other assets, such as bank accounts, mutual funds, stock, and investment real estate that don't fit into the exempt categories are considered "countable" assets when determining Medicaid eligibility. Countable assets are considered available to pay for nursing home costs and must be spent down before you become eligible for Medicaid. You have to pay the bill before the state does.

However, there are limitations on how you can list an auto or principal residence as a non-countable asset. For a single Medicaid recipient, the value of an auto cannot exceed $4,500 to be considered non-countable, although there is no limit on the value of an auto owned by a recipient's spouse.

The rules governing non-countable principal residences are a bit more complex. Your principal residence must be located in the same state in which you apply for Medicaid. As of 2005, your home equity must be less than $500,000 unless a spouse, minor, or disabled child lives there. Otherwise, equity above $500,000 is considered a countable asset. Specific guidelines regarding principal residence asset exemptions vary state to state. Also, the state may place a lien on your residence to recover the costs of your nursing home care that is revoked upon your death, with certain exemptions. In addition, some states require you to prove there is a reasonable chance that you will return home to exempt your house, while others (such as Massachusetts) only require that you "intend" to return home after your nursing home stay.

If your countable assets exceed Medicaid limits, you are not forever banned from enrolling in Medicaid. You must simply spend down your countable assets to the acceptable amount, meaning that the nursing home or long-term care provider will receive your assets until they are depleted to the point that Medicaid coverage kicks in.

PROTECTING YOUR ASSETS – THE FIVE YEAR RULE

If you have too many countable assets to qualify for Medicaid, you have two basic options: 1. Pay them down to a nursing home or other long-term care provider, or 2. Transfer them to your loved ones (or, in some instances, convert them into non-countable assets) to protect them. You can probably guess which options we strongly advise you take! Without careful financial planning, entering a nursing home can quickly turn into a major "lose the money" event.

One important factor to remember when you are preparing to protect your assets from nursing home costs is that Medicaid has a five-year "look-back" provision. Simply put, any asset transfer made within five years of entering a nursing home or other long-term care arrangement will be counted towards the determination of your Medicaid eligibility. These assets are still considered yours for a five-year period.

So if you place assets in an irrevocable trust and three years later have to enter a nursing home, those assets will still be considered countable and have to be spent down (i.e., paid to the nursing home for two years) before you can enroll in Medicaid. This five-year look-back period also applies to gifts or sales of assets at below market value. For example, if you transferred $90,000 to your grandchildren for college tuition and four years later had to enter a nursing home, you would not be eligible for Medicaid to cover your costs. You would have to pay the $90,000 towards your nursing home care. When we said you need to begin planning now, we weren't kidding!

Like any other rule, the five-year look-back rule has a few exceptions. New Medicaid regulations require each state to develop "hardship waivers" to allow exemptions within the five-year period. In addition, you can transfer assets at any time to a spouse, child under 21, blind or disabled child, child who has lived with you and provided care for at least two years, sibling who is a part-owner of your home and has lived there at least one year, or trust for a disabled person under 65.

PROTECTING YOUR ASSETS – IRREVOCABLE TRUSTS AND TESTAMENTARY TRUSTS – IF YOU DON'T OWN IT, THEY CAN'T GET IT

Let's assume you decide to protect your assets from being counted against your Medicaid eligibility well ahead of time. What is your best means of doing so? Outside of simply selling your assets off, donating them to charity, or transferring them to loved ones, placing them in a trust is probably one of your best options (but not the only good one).

154

We will discuss the rules and advantages of trusts in detail in the next chapter, but for now will provide a general explanation of how you can put a trust to work protecting your assets in the event you need nursing home or other long-term care for more than 100 days. An irrevocable trust is a legal entity that allows you to hold and manage your assets with certain tax advantages and financial guarantees, both during and after your life. We like to think of them as "bulletproof boxes" that protect your assets from excessive taxes and other dangers, such as nursing home expenses.

There are a variety of trusts you can set up that give you varying degrees of flexibility and control during and/or after your lifetime. To properly safeguard assets that might otherwise become "countable" in the eyes of Medicaid, you need to place them in an irrevocable lifetime trust. You cannot remove any property or assets once they are placed in the trust, and any other terms (such as who you name as the trustee(s) and beneficiary(ies), etc.) also must remain fixed. There are some exceptions that can be built into these types of trusts—we call them "escape hatches."

By creating your irrevocable trust as "income only," you forego access to the principal inside it. That means the principal, which in this case is made up of assets that would otherwise count against your Medicaid eligibility, is now non-countable. As a further benefit, the principal will pass directly to your beneficiaries after your death, bypassing probate and also reducing the chance the state will try to recoup Medicaid charges from your estate. Any income created by the trust will still be countable for Medicaid purposes. You pay income tax on all income distributed to you.

If you have a spouse who needs nursing home care, you can set up a testamentary trust, which is a trust that forms as part of your will after your estate passes through probate, to directly pay for their care services without affecting their Medicaid eligibility. There is no look-back period in a testamentary trust.

PROTECTING YOUR ASSETS – LIFE ESTATE

One way to ensure that your home does not wind up being used to finance a nursing home stay is to place it in an Irrevocable Life Estate Trust. As mentioned in Chapter 5, a Life Estate allows you to retain the use of your home while directing the remainder to pass to someone else when you die without going through probate or paying estate recovery charges. A Life Estate is still subject to the five-year look-back rule and the $500,000 home equity limit.

Also keep in mind that creating a Life Estate may create gift-tax liabilities and that once you place property in a Life Estate, you cannot sell it without approval of the named beneficiaries or engage in "wasteful" use of the property (i.e., use that damages or devalues it).

Just Don't Lose the Money Tip
Pre-Plan

A pre-plan is where you start planning on removing assets out of your name in order to protect those assets. Make sure you trust the trustee, and that any asset transfer does not affect your everyday life. A good trustee should think like you and if possible have more money than you—so that they are not tempted to take advantage of the situation.

PROTECTING YOUR ASSETS – LONG-TERM CARE INSURANCE

As discussed in the previous chapter, private long-term care insurance covers the cost of long-term medical care in the event you need to enter a nursing home, assisted living facility, hospice, rehabilitation center, or another long-term care facility. It may also cover the cost of qualified home healthcare services.

For retirees, private long-term care insurance acts as a supplement to Medicare after the 100-day coverage period runs out. Long-term care insurance still usually only covers a stay in a nursing home or other facility for a fixed period of time with a maximum monthly payment.

For these reasons, long-term care insurance can be useful as a tool to defray costs during the look-back period or to cover the costs of care related to prolonged illnesses, but on its own is generally not enough to completely cover you from losing the money. Long-term care insurance gives you money to buy time to get assets out of your name—remember, you need five years due to the look-back period. Before purchasing any long-term care insurance policy, make sure it is inflation-adjustable and provides enough coverage. Ideally, it should offer at least five years of coverage to protect any assets that may slip through the five-year look-back period. Most importantly, make sure you can afford whatever coverage you get. It is better to have a 70% solution that you can afford to sustain than a 100% solution that you might have to cancel if the premium goes up.

157

PROTECTING YOUR ASSETS – UNIVERSAL LIFE INSURANCE WITH LONG-TERM CARE BENEFIT

As noted in Chapter 9, a new type of universal life insurance (several companies offer this type of plan) provides coverage for long-term care. It offers a long-term care benefit for nursing home care, at-home care, assisted living, or adult day care. The coverage can be for as long as seven years. However, if you do not require long-term care, your heirs will receive a death benefit that is tax-free. The best part is that if you choose to cancel the policy you get your premium back. Unlike traditional long-term care policies, this type of universal life policy gives you life insurance, an investment component with tax-deferred growth, and provision for your long-term care if necessary. This type of policy is a single premium payment policy with lifetime guaranteed coverage and a premium that will never increase.

PROTECTING YOUR ASSETS – LIFE-CARE ANNUITIES

As a result of tax law changes stemming from the federal Pension Protection Act of 2006, a number of combined annuity-long-term care insurance products will become more viable as both tax-advantaged investments and vehicles to help pay for long-term care starting in 2010. Although the tax benefits do not take effect until Jan. 1, 2010, many insurers are already ramping up their offerings of these products and it is never too early to make an investment to help ensure a comfortable future.

Among the best of these products for the *Just Don't Lose the Money* investor is the life-care annuity, which for a single premium provides both a regular monthly post-retirement income and the guarantee of an increased disability payment in the event long-term care becomes a necessity. It also provides the cash value of an annuity, something most long-term care policies do not offer.

Even without the tax benefits scheduled to take effect in 2010, a life-care annuity can offer all the protection afforded by a separate irrevocable annuity and long-term care insurance policy, for a single premium that will most likely be more cost-efficient. And once 2010 rolls around, qualified withdrawals from life-care annuities will be exempt from income tax consideration. In addition, the holder of a life-care annuity will be able to exchange it for a long-term care insurance policy tax-free, allowing much greater flexibility to respond to major life events. Sound complicated? Well, it is, but it works.

PROTECTING YOUR ASSETS – CRISIS PLANNING

If you find yourself or your spouse unexpectedly needing nursing home care and you have not had time to properly protect your assets, you are not necessarily doomed to spending down all your hard-earned savings. In most states, you can use assets to purchase an annuity for the stay-at-home spouse at any time without affecting your Medicaid eligibility.

To meet Medicaid exemption standards, an annuity must be irrevocable so that the stay-at-home spouse cannot make any withdrawals beyond scheduled monthly payments. If you are married and an annuity of this type is purchased for the healthy, stay-at-home spouse, the beneficiary can be your children. The state must be named a remainder beneficiary for the amount of nursing home care provided if you are a single individual. While this option doesn't provide complete asset protection, it does allow Medicaid coverage to begin immediately, thereby reducing your own nursing home care expenses and leaving more money for your beneficiaries in the form of income from the annuity.

In addition, a reverse mortgage can be useful in situations where you did not have time to plan in advance. A reverse mortgage allows you to turn your home equity into cash in the form of monthly payments. You can use proceeds from a reverse mortgage to help pay for nursing home costs and qualify for Medicaid if the value of your home exceeds the $500,000 home equity limit.

Finally, you can also finance the purchase of non-countable assets, such as a home, auto, or prepaid funeral, with countable assets, which essentially converts otherwise countable assets into non-countable ones. This approach offers a better return on your "spend down" than simply forking your hard-earned cash over to a nursing home.

Estate Recovery

"Estate recovery" allows the state Medicaid program to seek reimbursement for nursing home costs from your estate. Under federal law, states must attempt to recover money from your probate estate. However, they have the option of seeking to pursue estate recovery against assets that pass outside of probate, which provides an added reason to avoid probate. If you're married, the state can't begin the estate recovery process until the death of the healthy spouse.

OTHER TYPES OF LONG-TERM CARE

While this chapter primarily deals with how not to lose your money to nursing home expenses, there are other forms of long-term care you also need to protect your assets against. Hospice care refers to residential care offered to those near the end of life. The focus is typically more on relieving pain and suffering than providing curative treatment.

Rehabilitation care can be on a residential or outpatient basis, and is geared toward assisting recovery from serious injury or illness. In-home health care is provided by nurses or home health aides and can be offered on a periodic or 24-hour basis, depending on severity of patient need.

Just Don't Lose the Money Tip
Control vs. Protection of Assets

Planning to protect assets from the high costs of nursing homes is very complicated and should be approached with caution. Many times you are trading control of an asset for the protection of that asset.

By placing assets in certain types of trusts, you give up control of the asset. This means you cannot directly access or sell the asset. But if you can access or sell the asset then that asset must be taken if you go into a nursing home. If you can't access it—they can't access it. Giving up control of some assets at some point in your life is not a bad idea as long as it does not change your lifestyle.

None of these types of medical care are cheap, and all are governed by Medicare and Medicaid rules similar to those governing nursing home care. When protecting your assets, keep the possibility in mind that you or your spouse may need other forms of long-term care in addition to or instead of nursing home care.

A QUICK REVIEW

1 Medicare will only cover 100 days' worth of nursing home or long-term care. After that, you must rely on Medicaid, an insurance plan offered jointly by the federal and state governments, to pay for your care. Medicaid has fairly stringent asset requirements and will require you to "spend down" excess assets before you qualify.

2 When applying for Medicaid, your assets are divided into "countable" and "non-countable" assets. Your goal should be to get as many of your assets as possible into the non-countable category or transfer them at least five years before you require nursing home or long-term care, as Medicaid has a five-year "look-back" policy. Viable options include placing countable assets in an irrevocable trust, placing your home in a Life Estate, obtaining long-term care insurance, or purchasing an irrevocable annuity.

3 You should protect your assets against the possibility of nursing home or long-term care long before you think you may need it. Consider some of the new financial options with your financial advisor such as universal life insurance with a long-term care

162

benefit and life-care annuities, which provide increased payments in the event of disability. Also keep Medicaid eligibility in mind when making other financial decisions. For example, if you place money in a trust to pay for a grandchild's education and then have to enter a nursing home within five years, that money will be considered as a countable asset even though you receive no direct financial benefit from it.

Just Don't Lose the Money Tip
Plan in Stages

Realistically, it would be extremely difficult to protect all your assets against nursing home expenses at once. The best way to go about shielding your assets from being counted toward Medicaid eligibility is to plan in stages, handling your most valuable assets first. For most people, this means starting with any real estate holdings and then moving on to other investments such as bank CDs, stock, and bond holdings.

To literally avoid "losing the money," an irrevocable trust may be your best option. You will protect the assets you have built up and only risk the interest. At later stages of your life, maintaining principal and having an income stream becomes a far greater priority than growing a portfolio, making an irrevocable trust an excellent asset protection plan for the careful investor.

Don't Lose the Money When You Die!
Avoiding Estate and Inheritance Taxes
and Related Costs and Problems

It has always been said there are only two certainties in life—death and taxes. Well, death we cannot avoid, but taxes we can avoid! With time and proper planning taxes can be avoided. The key to avoiding taxes is motivation. Are you motivated enough to make the necessary changes to avoid taxes? Some are and some aren't. Once someone said to me, "I don't mind paying taxes as much as I mind what the government is doing with my money." Well, if that is your motivation, there are strategies to reduce or eliminate taxes. Use them.

While some of the preceding chapters have touched upon the steps you need to take to ensure that you don't lose the money after you die, the majority of the advice we have given so far pertains to keeping the money during your lifetime. In this chapter, we will focus squarely on the importance of protecting your assets for your loved ones after you're gone.

As the old saying goes, the two sure things in life are death and taxes. We'd like to modify that cliché to include a third sure thing: If you don't take the proper advance steps, your death will be the biggest tax event of your life.

ESTATE PLANNING

What do you want to happen to your assets after you die? Do you want to leave ownership of all your money, property, and valuables up in the air, unprotected from combined federal and state tax bills that could reach 60 percent? Most likely not, or you wouldn't have bothered reading a book like this in the first place.

With some careful estate planning, you can avoid this scenario. Estate planning ensures that your estate is protected from undue taxes, avoids probate, and is given out in the way you want it to be given out. It's actually not as complex as it sounds, although consulting the appropriate financial and legal professionals is an absolute must. We will begin our estate planning overview with a look at the estate taxes that can make your demise such an expensive proposition.

ESTATE TAXES

No matter where you are residing in the United States at the time of your death, your estate is subject to the federal estate tax. Many states, but not all, also impose their own estate taxes. Since we do not have the space to go through the estate tax rules of each individual state, we will focus on the federal estate tax in this chapter. Consult a qualified professional familiar with estate tax rules of your state to obtain more information about any state-tax liabilities your estate may incur.

The Massachusetts Estate Tax

Because we are based in Massachusetts, we will briefly discuss the Massachusetts estate tax. Starting in 2006, Massachusetts law provides for a $1 million estate tax exclusion. This means that estates in Massachusetts do not have to pay the Massachusetts estate tax if the total value of the assets owned at death are less than $1 million. Estates worth more than $1 million are subject to the Massachusetts estate tax. Computation of the tax is based on the federal estate tax credit for state death taxes. This system is somewhat complex, but here is a brief example. If a person in Massachusetts died in 2008 and their total assets (known as the "gross estate") minus deductions are worth $1.5 million, the estate would owe about $64,000 in taxes to Massachusetts (about 4 percent of the total).

The federal estate tax is based on the value of all property you transfer at the time of your death. The tax is paid by your estate before it is distributed to your beneficiaries, although any assets used to pay off estate expenses (such as lawyers or funeral costs) or debts are deducted from the taxable amount.

To get an idea of what you could wind up owing the federal government when you die, get an estimate of your gross estate. This is the total fair market value of all the assets and property exclusively in your name at the time of your death. This includes real estate, autos, stocks, bonds, mutual funds, insurance (including insurance transferred within three years prior to your death), annuities (except for straight life annuities, see Chapter 2), 401(k)/IRAs, life estate property (see Chapter 5), and 50 percent of property jointly-owned with a spouse.

As mentioned previously, estate expenses and liabilities are exempt from estate tax. In addition, you can pass an unlimited amount of assets to a surviving spouse tax-free (we will discuss the potential disadvantages of this type of transfer shortly) and also transfer assets to an IRS-approved charity tax-free.

Estate tax rates are not static. They currently range from 41 to 46 percent of your gross estate. There is also an Estate Tax Credit whose value changes year to year, and if you die in 2010, your beneficiaries will luck out because that particular year there is no federal estate tax at all! The Estate Tax Credit is the total amount an individual can pass free of tax at death to all other beneficiaries except for his or her spouse (recall that you can pass an unlimited amount to your spouse tax-free). Congress will probably be adjusting the amount of this credit in the near future.

THE CREDIT FOR ESTATE AND GIFT TAXES IS INCREASED

For 2008, the Estate Tax Credit exempts the first $2,000,000 of wealth transfers made at death. This amount will increase as follows:

Year	Estate Tax Exemption	Maximum Tax Rates
2008	$2 million	45%
2009	$3.5 million	45%
2010	n/a (taxes repealed)	35% (gift-tax only)
2011 & Beyond	$1 million	55%

Sample Calculation: To see the estate tax in action, let's look at a sample calculation based on 2008 tax rates.

A single man named Tom owns the following property at the time of his death:

House	$800,000
Bank Account	$100,000
Stocks	$300,000
Bonds	$400,000
Life Insurance	$1,000,000
Total Gross Estate	$2,600,000

Because there are deductions that factor into the estate tax equation, Tom's estate doesn't have to pay taxes on this gross amount. The following items can be deducted from Tom's estate:

Donations to Charity	$100,000
Mortgage Debt	$75,000
Funeral Costs	$15,000
Lawyer Fees	$10,000
Total Deductions	$200,000 *

Gross Estate	$2,600,000
Deductions	-$200,000
Estate Tax Credit	-$2,000,000
Taxable Estate	$400,000
Estate Tax	$184,000 **

* This $200,000 would be deducted from Tom's gross estate to produce a final taxable amount of $2.4 million.

** Based on the prevailing IRS estate tax rates, an estate worth $2.4 million would owe $184,000 in taxes after the $2 million Estate Tax Credit is deducted from the total.

Keep in mind that a married couple is allowed one federal estate tax credit and one state estate tax credit for each individual. However, if you leave all your assets to your spouse tax-free, once your spouse dies and those assets pass to your children, they will lose your Estate

Tax Credit. As a result, they will pay taxes on the full amount as demonstrated in Example 1.

Example 1:
Everything Going to Surviving Spouse

Suppose Jack and Diane are married and have the following assets:

House	$1.1 million
Bank Account	$200,000
Stocks	$500,000
Bonds	$800,000
Life Insurance	$1 million
Annuities	$800,000
Total Gross Estate	$4.4 million

Husband died in 2006, left everything to wife.
No estate tax due – marital deduction.

Gross Estate	$4.4 million
Marital Deduction	–$4.4 million
Taxable Estate	$0
Estate Tax	$0

Wife dies in 2008, leaves everything to kids. Wife gets estate tax credit ($2 million in 2008), but her estate still owes tax on remaining $2.4 million. Estate tax due is $1.1 million or 25%.

Gross Estate	$4.4 million
Estate Tax Credit	– $2.0 million
Taxable Estate	$2.4 million
Estate Tax	$1.1 million

One way to avoid this scenario is to leave assets up to the estate tax credit amount to your children and the remainder to your spouse. You can also use a variety of trusts to get around this "one-shot" estate tax credit provision (see the section on trusts later on in this chapter).

Furthermore, if you skip a generation in transferring your assets (i.e. directly leave assets to grandchildren), there is a tax on any assets worth more than $1 million, added onto the existing estate tax.

After subtracting all allowable deductions and the Estate Tax Credit from your estate value, you can determine what assets you will have to pay taxes on. Fortunately, there are ways to mitigate your estate tax bill, which we will discuss soon.

WILLS

A will is a legally binding document that allows you to control the distribution of your assets after your death. A will covers the distribution of any assets that are subject to probate (see below), and does not cover assets that are held in a trust, jointly-held, or in life insurance policies. Rules governing wills vary from state to state; some states are very lenient about exactly what type of document constitutes a binding will, while other states have stringent guidelines you must follow.

There are many good reasons to have an updated will that specifically covers the distribution of all your major assets. This should include specific bequests for individual assets of great monetary or sentimental value, such as antiques or heirlooms, as well as broader assets such as real estate holdings and bank accounts.

In addition to ensuring that your money stays in the family, a will can also minimize tax liabilities, allow you to appoint an executor to manage your estate (more on this when we cover probate), designate a guardian for any minor children, and minimize the length and expense of probate proceedings (see below).

If you die without a will, a probate court will determine how to divide your assets, who will act as executor, and even who will serve as guardian for any minor children. Your estate will also likely be subject to the maximum allowable federal and state taxes.

In addition to a will, it's also a good idea to create a durable power of attorney document to designate someone to manage and distribute your assets in the event you become incompetent or incapacitated due to illness or injury during your lifetime. A person holding durable power of attorney has full access to and control over all your assets, including your bank accounts and property holdings.

Why give someone so much power in the event you become incapacitated? Because if you don't choose someone and the worst happens, your family has to go through the time and expense of having the court appoint a guardian or conservator, and they may not select the same person you would.

You can grant durable power of attorney to someone immediately or in the event of your incapacitation. You can specify how to determine if you're incapacitated and revoke the durable power of attorney at any time through written notification. Naturally, you should only designate someone who is extremely trustworthy and qualified, and you should never create a will or durable power of attorney document without professional assistance and careful forethought and planning.

PROBATE

When your estate enters probate, a state court clears title on your property so that it can properly pass to the beneficiaries named in your will, or distributed according to the state laws of intestacy in the event you don't have a will. The probate process begins with your will being filed with the court and your executor being appointed. The executor is the person you choose to manage the distribution of your assets according to the terms of the will and make sure that any unpaid debts or taxes are settled. The executor can be a relative, friend, or hired professional.

After the will is filed and the executor is appointed, the probate court will collect and inventory all your assets, and then hold them until it is ready to authorize your executor to distribute them. The executor must ensure that any estate taxes or unpaid debts are paid off before anything passes to your beneficiaries. Finally, the court will allow distribution of any remaining assets, with the executor required to provide a final account listing all expenses and distributions.

If you own an asset by yourself, it is most likely subject to probate. This includes tangible assets such as real estate and intangible assets such as royalty rights. Jointly-owned property immediately passes to the co-owner, avoiding probate. Assets where you are the named beneficiary, such as a 401(k) plan, IRA, life insurance, or annuity, also avoid probate. Avoiding probate is not a guarantee of avoiding estate taxes (more on those in a moment).

So what's so bad about probate, anyway? First, it loses some of the money from your estate. Probate incurs a variety of fees, expenses, and costs that all come out of the estate before your beneficiaries see a dime. Second, probate usually takes about a year to complete—delaying your beneficiaries' inheritance, and it also drags out the entire process of your loved ones coming to terms with your death and moving forward. Third, all probate documents are a matter of public record, eliminating any privacy your beneficiaries may have about what they're inheriting, or even any personal privacy you may want to maintain after you're deceased.

Just Don't Lose the Money Tip
Avoiding Probate Will Avoid Costs

TRUSTS

A trust is a legal entity that allows you to hold and manage assets, during or after your lifetime, with protection from certain tax liabilities. We have referred to trusts a number of times throughout this book, so as you may imagine, we are big fans of trusts! As noted earlier, we like to think of a trust as a "bulletproof box" against taxes and any unnecessary delays (such as probate) in getting assets to your beneficiaries after your death.

You can place ownership of any tangible or intangible assets into a trust. While the trust then becomes the "owner" of these assets, the assets are held for your benefit or the benefit of anyone you designate. A trust is managed by one or more trustees, who look after the assets, handle any investments, and manage the distribution schedule you create.

Trustees can be individuals or corporate fiduciaries (such as a bank you pay to manage your trust). You can name yourself as trustee, although this can expose your estate to taxes. Any trustee is legally obligated to act in the best interest of named trust beneficiaries.

One of the best reasons for creating a trust is that it gives you a way of directly passing assets along to your beneficiaries after you die, without going through probate. You can also control how your beneficiaries receive your assets, which can protect against estate taxes, creditors, and simple human nature if you have a beneficiary with poor financial management skills.

There are a variety of trusts you can establish to help ensure you just don't lose the money after you die. We will examine several of the significant types of trusts you can create.

TESTAMENTARY TRUST

A testamentary trust is established in a will and comes into effect during probate. You do not have to fund the trust or pay any administrative fees while you're alive, which reduces the cost significantly. The major drawback to a testamentary trust is that it does not help your estate avoid probate.

LIVING TRUST: REVOCABLE AND IRREVOCABLE

A living or "inter vivos" trust is created and funded during your lifetime. The trust takes ownership of any assets you place inside, placing them outside of your probate estate. There are two types of living trust to choose from: revocable and irrevocable.

With a revocable living trust, you retain direct control over any assets you place inside. You can remove them or spend them as you wish, and you can fund a living revocable trust after your death with a "pour over" will. Assets in a revocable living trust pass directly to your beneficiaries without going through probate, but are subject to estate taxes since you essentially remain as their owner.

Furthermore, placing certain kinds of stock or stock options, as well as IRAs, pension plans, and/or real estate, in a revocable living trust may cause negative tax implications. Always consult a qualified financial professional before transferring assets to a revocable living trust, or any type of trust, for that matter.

Unlike a revocable living trust, an irrevocable living trust does not offer you any flexibility with or direct control over the assets you

177

place inside. Assets cannot be removed or amended once they are transferred to an irrevocable living trust. By surrendering control over these assets, you exclude them from estate taxes as well as probate, although gift taxes may still apply. There is also protection from attachment or lien if a nursing home is needed (see Chapter 10).

IRREVOCABLE LIFE INSURANCE TRUST (ILIT)

You can enhance your estate tax savings by placing a life insurance policy into an irrevocable living trust, creating what is known as an irrevocable life insurance trust, or ILIT. An ILIT enables you to remove the proceeds of a life insurance policy from the estate tax and also manage them after your death.

To create an ILIT, you can either transfer an existing life insurance policy into an irrevocable living trust or have the trustee purchase a policy in your name with trust proceeds. You then pay the premiums by transferring money into the trust. Any gift tax the policy incurs will be based on its value at the time of transfer rather than its value at the time of your death. Keep in mind that if you die within three years of transferring a life insurance policy into a trust, the policy's proceeds are still subject to estate tax. As discussed in Chapter 9, an ILIT can also be used for wealth replacement in the event you require long-term care or make gifts to charity.

CREDIT SHELTER TRUST

A credit shelter trust is a type of revocable living trust that allows a married couple to protect its federal estate tax exemption. If you are a married couple whose combined estate is equal to or greater than the current estate tax credit amount, a credit shelter trust may make sense for you (and your beneficiaries).

Simply put, the credit shelter trust preserves your estate tax credit for whatever money remains outside the trust. In a sense, you get to use the estate tax credit twice, since the trust automatically shelters an asset amount equivalent to the credit and then allows you to apply it to the rest of your estate. Depending on the size of your estate, this can virtually eliminate the estate tax as shown in Example 2.

Example 2:
Tax Efficient Plan—Utilizing Husband's Estate Tax Credit

Husband died in 2006, preserves his estate tax credit by using Credit Shelter Trust and gives remainder outright to wife.

Husband's Gross Estate	$4.4 million
Marital Deduction	−$2.4 million
Estate Tax Credit	$ 2.0 million (put in Credit Shelter Trust for wife's benefit)
Taxable Estate	$0
Estate Tax	$0

When wife dies in 2008, the amount in Credit Shelter Trust is not included in her gross estate and passes directly to kids free of tax.

Estate tax due is $184,000 or 4.18%—a savings of $916,000 had they not used a Credit Shelter Trust (see Example 1).

Wife's Gross Estate	$2.4 million
Estate Tax Credit	−$2.0 million
Taxable Estate	$ 400,000
Estate Tax	$184,000

Typically, a credit shelter trust is funded at the death of the first spouse through a pour over will. The surviving spouse is permitted access to any income produced by the trust, as well as limited access to the principal for reasons such as health care and education. They are also allowed to withdraw up to 5 percent of the principal or $5,000, whichever is greater, for any reason.

CHARITABLE REMAINDER TRUST

In Chapter 9, we touched upon Charitable Remainder Trusts for wealth replacement and asset protection when combined with life insurance. A charitable remainder trust, which is an irrevocable living trust with a charity named as the beneficiary, is also a way for you to leave money to a charitable cause while obtaining tax advantages on the trust's investments while you're alive. You are allowed to use the proceeds from a Charitable Remainder Trust to create a lifetime income, although the principal remains inaccessible. The property within the trust is sold and reinvested to create a lifetime income for you. The income paid out is usually a fixed percentage of the assets held in the trust.

At the time of your death, all principal held by a Charitable Remainder Trust will go to the charity you named as beneficiary, so this is not a way to leave money to your heirs. However, if you are already planning to leave a tax-free bequest to a charity, this is a way to set that bequest aside ahead of time and gain some advantages from it. See Chapter 9 for details on how to create a Wealth Replacement Trust, which combines a Charitable Remainder Trust and a tax-free life insurance policy to replace assets that you used during your lifetime, which in turn reduced your wealth. Your estate can be reduced by taxes, long-term care costs, and/or gifts to charity, so you may want to look at wealth replacement options.

FUNERAL/INTERMENT PREPAYMENT

Funeral and interment expenses are exempt from estate taxes. To make things easier for your beneficiaries, you can set up provisions either in your will or in a life insurance policy to set aside money in advance to pay for your funeral and interment. Many funeral homes and cemeteries also have prepayment plans, which allow you to pay today's lower rates for tomorrow's higher-priced services and burial. Prepaying funeral and interment expenses is also an excellent way to help qualify for Medicaid without having to spend down your assets (see Chapter 10 for details).

A QUICK REVIEW

1 Without proper planning, when you die, your estate will have to pass through probate, a state court proceeding that can take up to a year, before being distributed to your beneficiaries. If you don't have an updated, legally valid will, the state will determine how your assets are distributed and who will become guardian of any minor children you may leave behind. Furthermore, unless you make financial preparations, your estate may be subject to heavy estate taxes before your loved ones receive anything.

2 Your gross estate is subject to federal (and possibly state) estate taxes. This is the total fair market value of all the assets and property exclusively in your name at the time of your death, including real estate, autos, stocks, bonds, mutual funds, insurance (including insurance transferred within three years prior to your death), annuities (except for straight life annuities), 401(k)/IRAs, life estate property, and 50 percent of property jointly-owned with a spouse. Your estate is eligible to receive a federal and state estate tax credit, although you can lose the credit if you leave everything to a surviving spouse.

3 Assets placed in a trust pass directly to the named beneficiaries without having to go through probate. Assets placed in an irrevocable living trust are also exempt from estate taxes, although gift taxes may still apply. There are a variety of trusts you can create that can protect your assets, estate tax credit, life insurance policy, and/or charitable donations.

Just Don't Lose the Money Tip
Use Your Estate Tax Credit Wisely!

Your estate receives a single federal estate tax credit and where applicable, a single state estate tax credit. If you don't use them, you lose them, but you don't want to waste them, either!

If you are a single person, you can simply apply the estate tax credit to your estate at the time of your death and that pretty much covers it. But if you're married, the estate tax credit gets trickier. You can pass any amount of assets to your spouse tax-free, but unless you protect your estate tax credit, it will disappear in the process. You need to either directly leave children or other beneficiaries an amount of assets equal to the estate tax credit, or create a credit shelter trust that preserves the estate tax credit while still creating income for your surviving spouse.

Above All, Just Don't Lose the Money!

Summary/Conclusion

Congratulations! You have completed your crash course in how not to lose the savings you spent a lifetime accumulating. But before you go off to put the lessons of this book into practice, we'd like to leave you with a few parting thoughts. Don't worry, we won't take too long, and we won't charge you anything extra, either.

Most importantly, remember that *Just Don't Lose the Money* is an entire mindset based around following simple rules to prevent putting your wealth at risk. It encompasses both legal and financial strategies. Losing money in the stock market because there is no diversification in your portfolio, and losing money because your estate goes through probate is the same dollar lost.

The first step to not losing the money is determining what you actually have to lose. You'd be surprised how easy it is to lose something when you don't even realize you have it in the first place. So begin by taking a thorough accounting of your net worth, which is the sum total of all your assets and income sources, minus your annual expenses and liabilities.

Also take potential future expenses such as healthcare and education of children and grandchildren into account. Hopefully you are left with a positive number that is well above zero!

Now that you have an idea of what there is to lose, it's time to determine what you want to do with it. Do you want to leave everything to the kids and spend nothing on yourself, or do you want to spend your remaining days spending everything on a life of luxury? Odds are your plans will fall somewhere between these extremes, but until you set out a concrete list of post-retirement goals, you will not be able to create a plan that will adequately serve your individual needs.

Regardless of your specific goals and needs, when designing your investment strategies, you will want to err on the side of asset protection, rather than growth. At this stage in your life, you will have far less opportunity to make back anything you lose, which is why you need to take a more conservative investment outlook. Certainly some risks are acceptable, but a steady, moderate return is what you're looking for, not a variable return with high potential risks and rewards.

Putting It All Together: Asset Allocation Strategies

When creating your investment portfolio, you need to allocate assets to cover three key areas: basic expenses, catastrophic expenses, and estate tax protection. A brief overview of each area follows:

Basic Allocation for Basic Expenses

Basic expenses, the day-to-day costs of everyday life such as food, clothing, shelter and routine entertainment, are best covered by basic investments such as bank accounts, stocks, bonds, mutual funds, and annuities. You will want a mix of fixed-return investments such as bank accounts and fixed annuities, and variable-return investments such as stocks and mutual funds. Having a core account that provides most of your basic expenses is the safest way to go.

When selecting variable return investments, carefully assess the amount of risk you're taking. A proven blue chip stock or mutual fund that invests in blue chips is a much better long-term investment than a stock of a new company in a hot new sector that could dramatically rise or fall at any time. And you're definitely planning for the long-term here.

Also keep the "hidden costs" of any of these investments in mind before putting any of your hard-earned money into them. Hidden costs include fees, taxes, service charges, and other expenditures that may not be readily apparent. For example, a mutual fund that has a high "churn" (rate of buying and selling stocks and/or bonds in the fund) will incur more trading fees than a fund with a low churn. To find out about a fund's expenses and expense ratios, you will need to do a little independent research before investing in it.

Just Don't Lose the Money Tip
Always Consult a Professional!

You probably noticed that we repeated various versions of the statement, "Always consult a qualified financial (or legal) professional," about 5,000 times during the course of this book. Or at least it probably seemed like 5,000 times. There is a reason we repeated this advice so often—it's an absolute requirement!

Financial investment is an extremely complex and risky endeavor. The purpose of this book is to explain the basics to you and provide you with the tools to determine how much you have to save and what you need to save it for. Armed with this information, you can have an intelligent conversation with the appropriate professionals to design a portfolio that best meets your unique goals and needs.

Understanding the basics of health care makes you a more informed patient who can better explain what you need to a doctor, but you would not diagnose and treat your own medical condition. Similarly, understanding the basics of finance makes you a more informed investor who can better explain what you need to a planner or other financial professional, but you would not create your own portfolio without qualified advice.

Don't be afraid to shop around for a financial planner. Ask for references, obtain names from friends and relatives with successful portfolios, and research a planner's overall investment performance. In the end, the final decision on how to invest always rests with you, but shouldn't that decision be as well-informed as possible?

CATASTROPHIC EXPENSES – NURSING HOME PROTECTION

The old adage "hope for the best, prepare for the worst" is one the *Just Don't Lose the Money* investor should live by. Naturally, you are planning for a pleasant, carefree retirement that will truly qualify as your "golden years." Hopefully, these plans will become reality. But we all know that reality doesn't always go according to plan.

As you age, the prospect of needing long-term healthcare, and possibly even permanent nursing home care, becomes greater. According to the American Society on Aging, people have a 70 percent chance of needing some type of long-term care after age 65. Without proper planning, the costs associated with long-term healthcare and nursing home care will destroy savings of almost any size.

Unless you have post-retirement healthcare coverage provided by a pension, working spouse or other means, make sure you put money aside to pay for Medicare and Medigap insurance coverage. The free Part A coverage provided by Medicare is a nice feature of Social Security, but by itself is not enough to adequately protect you against the kind of healthcare bills that can arise as you get older.

You also need to be prepared for the possibility of needing nursing home care beyond the 100 days provided for by Medicare. While the government offers the Medicaid program to help pay for nursing home and other long-term care, its stringent financial requirements mean you have to either spend down your hard-earned savings or find ways to turn your "countable" assets into "non-countable" assets.

Start investigating ways you can protect your assets, such as placing your home in a Life Estate, investing in an annuity, or creating an income-only irrevocable trust, now. You should also consider some of the new financial products with your financial advisor that have been developed for this purpose. There is universal life insurance with a long-term care benefit that offers an accelerated death benefit to pay for long term care if needed. In addition, there are life-care annuities, which provide increased payments in the event of disability. There are guaranteed lifetime income products available that do not require giving up your principal. In short, the financial services industry has responded to the long-term income and health care needs of a society that is living longer. Medicaid has a five-year "look-back" provision that limits what kinds of steps you can take to protect your assets within five years of entering a nursing home or other long-term care arrangement. That means you need to be prepared for this possibility well before you ever think it may happen.

ESTATE PROTECTION – SAVING ESTATE TAXES AND AVOIDING PROBATE EXPENSES

Dying can be one of the most expensive things you ever do. Even taking the relatively generous estate tax credit into account, federal and state taxes can still bite a huge chunk out of your estate before your beneficiaries ever see a dime. Probate costs can also add up. Fortunately, there are many ways to minimize your estate's exposure.

Trusts represent one of the best methods to reduce estate taxes. Any assets placed inside an irrevocable trust avoid both estate taxes and probate, while assets inside a revocable trust avoid probate but are subject to estate taxes. If you are married and plan to leave your estate to your surviving spouse before other beneficiaries receive anything, you should investigate options to protect your estate tax credit, such as creating a credit shelter trust.

To keep your home out of probate, you can place it in a Life Estate Trust, which technically transfers ownership to a named beneficiary but allows you to live there for the remainder of your life. However, the home is still part of your estate for tax purposes.

Another simple way to put assets out of the probate court and tax-man's way is to place them in a joint-and-survivor IRA Annuity, which is a lifetime annuity that starts paying a specified monthly amount when you turn 59 ½ and then continues payments to a surviving beneficiary. This can be done without giving up principal. To extend the benefit of your IRA Annuity, invest the payments in an Irrevocable Life Insurance Trust (ILIT), a type of trust that enables you to remove the proceeds of a life insurance policy from the estate tax and also manage them after your death. Placing a life insurance policy in an ILIT is a great estate tax saver and will enable you to avoid a big tax bite for your loved ones.

FINAL THOUGHTS

The best part of the *Just Don't Lose the Money* investment philosophy is that at heart it is a simple, pragmatic approach to wealth management. One of the most important *Just Don't Lose the Money* tools you possess is your own common sense. You've been around a while, you know what it takes to earn and keep money; you've probably even been burned once or twice but are wiser for the experience.

All we are really asking you to do is take the same God-given common sense that has guided you throughout your working career and continue using it to guide you in your post-working career. If an investment opportunity comes along that seems too good to be true, surely you know that it most likely is. You probably did your homework when you were buying a car or purchasing a home, so why not apply that same tenacious research to discover hidden costs and fees of investments you are considering?

You don't need to be a financial expert to keep the money after you retire. You do need to educate yourself on the basics, obtain and follow advice from qualified professionals, and always listen to that little voice in your head that tells you when something is or isn't right. You were smart enough to come this far, surely you're smart enough to make it the rest of the way.

And if you're ever in doubt over a financial decision, remember one simple thing: JUST DON'T LOSE THE MONEY!

Glossary

401(k): Retirement savings plans that you contribute to through your employer. Plans through non-profit employers are called 403(b).

Annuity: A contract with an insurance company to receive periodic payments (income) for life or a term of years. The payments can be fixed or variable depending on the provisions in the contract. Certain annuities protect your principal with a guaranteed minimum rate of interest. (See also Fixed annuity; Fixed-index annuity; and Life-Care annuity).

Bonds: A written promise by a borrower to pay interest periodically and repay the principal when the bond matures. Bonds are typically offered by government agencies (e.g., savings bonds) or corporations.

Certificates of Deposit (CDs): An investment account where you agree to leave money with the bank for a specific period of time without withdrawing it, in return for a specified rate of interest.

Capital Gains: Profits earned from the sale of investments. These include sale of stocks, bonds, mutual funds, or houses.

Capital gains tax: A tax on capital gains, or profits earned from the sale of investments. These include sale of stocks, bonds, mutual funds, or houses.

Charitable Remainder Trust: An irrevocable living trust with a charity named as the beneficiary that allows you to use its proceeds to create a lifetime income while the principal remains inaccessible. At the time of your passing, the principal amount is given to the charity you named as beneficiary.

Depreciation: A decrease in value of a given object or investment.

Estate Recovery: Reimbursement for nursing home costs that Medicaid (government program) can claim against the assets in your estate. States must try to recover nursing home costs from your probate estate and they have the option of seeking recovery from assets that pass outside of probate.

Estate Tax: A tax based on the value of total property you own at the time of your death, which is paid from the value of the estate itself, before the assets and property are transferred to the beneficiaries.

Exchange Traded Funds (ETFs): Open-ended mutual funds that continually trade shares on the stock market with returns linked to an established stock market index, a specific market sector or commodity, or a proprietary index. ETFs typically feature lower expense ratios than traditional mutual funds and are traded on the stock market.

Executor: The person you choose to manage the distribution of your property when you die according to instructions you give in your will; the manager of your estate.

Five-Year Look-Back: A Medicaid provision that limits what kinds of steps you can take to protect (transfer) your assets within five years of entering a nursing home or other long-term care facility.

Fixed annuity: A contract with an insurance company that returns principal plus a preset interest rate.

Fixed-index annuity: An investment in an annuity whose returns are calculated based on growth in a particular index such as the S&P 500.

Gift-tax: A tax you pay when you transfer assets (e.g., property, money, stocks, bonds, jewelry) to someone else during your lifetime.

Individual Retirement Account (IRA): A personal retirement investment that allows an individual to contribute certain sums annually and receive special tax allowances. There are two types of IRA's: Traditional IRA and Roth IRA.

Irrevocable Life Insurance Trusts (ILIT): A type of trust to hold life insurance where beneficiaries pay no income or estate taxes on the proceeds, and it does not pass through probate. The cash from this type of trust can be paid as a lump sum, as interest only (the principal remains with the insurance company and can be withdrawn at will), as fixed installments with interest, or as life income based on the beneficiaries' age and amount of the proceeds. It can also be used for wealth replacement in the event you require long-term care or make gifts to charity.

Junk bonds: Bonds rated below BBB/Baa offering high yields but also a higher risk of default.

Kiddie-tax: An IRS requirement for children under 14 to pay their parents' tax rate (as opposed to their own lower child's tax rate) on all unearned income (such as bond interest) exceeding a specified level that is regularly adjusted.

Life-care annuity: An annuity that for a single premium provides both a regular monthly post-retirement income and the guarantee of an increased disability payment in the event long-term care becomes a necessity.

Life Estate: A type of ownership of real estate often used to avoid probate: ownership of the real estate terminates on the death of the owner and transfers directly to a named beneficiary on the deed.

Life Insurance: A lump sum paid at the time of your death that acts as a means of replacing the money you would have earned if you were still alive and working. The money paid out is subject to income tax but not to estate tax if it is put in an irrevocable trust.

Load: Fee charged by some mutual funds to join or leave.

Medicaid: A joint federal/state program that provides medical assistance to children, seniors, and disabled persons who meet income and asset requirements. It's a means-tested program limited only to those with financial need, often used for nursing home costs.

Medicare: A federal program that provides health coverage for seniors (citizens over 65). A high-interest, high-minimum-balance deposit account that is designed for savings, but allows the holder limited capability to write checks and perform other transfers.

Mutual funds: Accounts in which investors pool their money together to buy stocks, bonds, or other types of investments.

Net Asset Value (NAV): The total sum of all assets in a fund divided by the number of shares in the fund.

Principal: The amount you invest in a given asset or security.

Pour-Over Will: Provision in a will that distributes assets to a trust — the money will "pour over" into the trust.

Probate: A legal proceeding conducted by a state court that oversees and manages the distribution of your property after you die in order to clear title of ownership on your property, so that it can pass from you to your beneficiaries as dictated by your will or by the laws of intestacy, if you don't have a will.

Real Estate Investment Trust (REIT): An account where investors pool their ownership of multiple real estate properties by purchasing shares, similar to a mutual fund.

Reverse mortgage: An agreement where a bank or other financial institution takes your house as collateral on a loan and then releases the equity to you, either in a lump sum or in installments.

Simplified Employee Pension (SEP): A non-portable, tax-deferred vehicle that features flexible employee contributions but no employer matching agreement. These also include Employee Stock Ownership (ESOP) options.

Stocks: Shares of ownership in a company.

Trusts: A kind of holding-box that invests and distributes your assets for you and your beneficiaries; a legal entity that holds and manages your assets while you're alive or after you're dead. Often used to avoid probate.

Universal Life Insurance with Long-Term Care Benefit: A plan that offers not only life insurance, but also creates an opportunity for tax-deferred investment growth along with long-term care coverage should it become necessary.

Wealth Replacement: An investment strategy that involves purchasing life insurance and using it to replace assets used for long-term care, charitable donations, or estate taxes.

Will: A legal document that communicates your desires and intentions for the distribution of your property at your death. Can be revoked or amended during your lifetime.

Zero-coupon bonds: Bonds issued by the U.S. Treasury, municipalities, and corporations that pay the holder no interest until maturity.

About the Authors

RICHARD L. RUBINO, JD

Richard L. Rubino is a managing partner of Rubino & Liang, LLC, a full services firm located in Newton, MA. He is a member of the National Academy of Elder Law Attorneys and the Boston Estate Planning Council. He is a seven-time recipient of the Top of the Table Award, given by the Million Dollar Roundtable in recognition for great achievement within the financial services industry. Rich has also been named by the "Who's Who" registry as a member of the elite "Who's Who in Business Worldwide."

Rich was born and raised in Brooklyn, New York and settled in Brookline, Massachusetts after attending law school and volunteering for a year with Volunteers in Service to America (VISTA). He received his Juris Doctor (JD) degree from Suffolk University in 1969, and is a member of the Massachusetts, New York, and Florida Bar Associations. He advises his clients on legal matters and works with other attorneys who specialize in different fields of law. He and his wife, Winnie, have two children, Jamie and Ryan.

Samuel J. Liang

Samuel Liang is a managing partner at Rubino & Liang, LLC, a financial services firm located in Newton, MA. Some of Sam's past achievements include being the recipient of the 1999 Boston Business Journal's 40 Under 40 award. In 2000, he also received the prestigious Francis Lowell Cabot Award as the Alumni of the year for the University of Massachusetts-Lowell. He is a nine-time recipient of the Top of the Table Award, given by the Million Dollar Roundtable in recognition for great achievement within the financial services industry. Sam has also been named by the "Who's Who" registry as a member of the elite "Who's Who in Business Worldwide."

Born in Hong Kong, Sam came to this country in 1974. When he arrived he couldn't speak English. By the time he graduated high school, he ranked in the top 10% of his class. Sam and his wife Eileen live in Bedford with their four children, Devin, Samantha, Ethan, and Harrison.

Along with his partner Richard Rubino, Sam Liang co-hosts "Senior Financial Focus," the Boston-area syndicated financial talk show for seniors heard throughout Eastern Massachusetts every Sunday morning 9 a.m. to 10 a.m. on WRKO (680 AM).

Rubino&Liang,LLC

Rubino & Liang, LLC is a financial services firm that provides advice, products, and services primarily to retirement-aged clients in the Greater Boston area. From retirement and estate planning to wealth transfer and preservation strategies, the firm is highly focused on the needs of the pre-retirement and retired individual.

Rubino & Liang's innovative approach has earned its founders industry recognition as leaders in catering to the needs of the retired individual. Founders Richard Rubino, JD and Samuel Liang also host a successful radio talk show that provides seniors with information and insights into the unique financial challenges that face the retired individual.

With their clients they emphasize:

- Sound basic principles and common sense.
- Principal-protected accounts when appropriate.
- Asset allocations that have growth with emphasis on safety.
- Employing tax efficiency and/or tax deferral strategies.
- Protecting real estate and family heirlooms.
- Using trusts when appropriate for smooth transition to heirs.
- Reducing and/or eliminating probate and estate taxes.
- Protecting and preserving assets if nursing home is needed.

"My parents lived through the Depression, worked overtime to put me and my sisters through college, and uprooted their lives to move to America from Hong Kong so we could have a chance at a better life," says Sam. He often thinks about this, which drives him and gives him the passion to ensure a level of comfort for his parents during their retirement and the same dedication to all of his clients.

SERVICES OFFERED

As members of the National Academy of Elder Law Attorneys (NAELA) and members of the Boston Estate Planning Council (BEPC), Rich and Sam stay informed and current on any changes in the law. They specialize in asset preservation strategies for seniors over 50 years old:

- Investment recommendations for pre-retirees and post-retirees.
- Estate planning from basic wills to trust design.
- Asset protection for business owners to nursing home disasters.
- Inheritance planning and use of the *No Blood, No Money* technique.

There is a lot of information out there to choose from.

Call us to help you choose the best strategies for you at 877-630-8787.